MW00849586

MIRACLES, MOMENTUM AND MANIFESTATION

Unleash the Secret Powers to Having the Life You Desire

First Edition Anthology

Antoinette Sykes

and

Seven Contributors

MIRACLES, MOMENTUM AND MANIFESTATION

Unleash the Secret Powers to Having the Life You Desire

Advance Praise for Miracles, Momentum and Manifestation

I WOULD LIKE to thank you for writing this second book in the "Bounceback Series," *Miracles, Manifestation and Momentum*. The authors this time around have done it again —enlightened us about many areas of life that people face and are looking for a glimmer of hope to pull through their situation. Personally, it has helped me realign and set my sights on something brighter and serves as a reminder, that miracles are just as natural as breathing. Thanks for the reminders and sheer transparency.

~**Karen Adams**, M. A., Counselor for Montgomery County Public Schools

WITH MANY BOOKS on and about the topics of "creating the life you want" and "your thoughts change your life", it's refreshing to not only see the theory of the process; but sheer stories of tenacity and hope, with a genuine look at how to navigate the storms to see the miracles in the midst and on the other side. Thank you for your truths.

Sharon Zhamalu, Entrepreneur | Z-Consulting

Dedication

THIS BOOK IS dedicated to you if you are searching for a better way. Simply pause, look in the mirror, realize you are *One With God* and there begins your answer.

Know the Truth and Truth will set you free.

~John 8:32

Acknowledgements

AS A WOMAN and business owner this series of books is a dream come true—becoming an author and a best selling one, at that.

Many thanks to God for speaking to me so clearly; I love you.

My family and friends are simply the best. Know that your love, laughter and firm words of wisdom land warmly in my heart. For that, I am forever grateful for being connected. I genuinely like you and unabashedly love you.

To the miracles I have yet to meet, I know you're on the way. I'm simply giddy with love and expectation.

My literary team is a rock; that's all. Thank you.

x

Table of Contents

ADVANCE PRAISE FOR MIRACLES, MOMENTUM AND MANIFESTATION ....

DEDICATION ....

ACKNOWLEDGEMENTS ....

INTRODUCTION ....

UNLEASE THE SECRET POWERS TO HAVING THE LIFE YOU DESIRE ....

ANTOINETTE SYKES 1

Can You Relate?...

Supernaturally You.....

The Natural Way of Miracles ....

Angel...

About the Author ....

LEARNING TO LISTEN ....

AMBER J. BOSWELL 11

My Story..

Where Does It Begin?...

Life's Lessons Follow Us..

Finding Beauty in the Dimmed Light of Shattered Dreams ....

Adding Momentum to Manifesting Dreams.....................

Listening for the Miracles.. 26

About the Author.. 30

BREAKDOWN TO BREAKTHROUGH **33**

MARY CANTY MERRILL, PH.D..33

Introduction 33

The Back Story 36

Repressed Feelings and Emotions..................................... 37

Psychotherapy 39

Breakdown – Reduced to Ashes... 40

Breakthrough – A Spiritual Renaissance........................... 44

Knocked Down, but Not Out.. 46

Symptoms of Depression.. 47

Causes of Depression 47

Treatment Options and Sources.. 48

A Divine Appointment and Full-Circle Moment............. 49

Each Day is an Opportunity to Begin Anew...................... 53

About the Author.. 56

THE MIRACLE OF MAN-I-FESTING THE ULTIMATE LOVE RELATIONSHIP! **59**

MAMIKO ODEGARD, PH.D...59

Create the Best Version of Yourself; be EXTRA-ordinary... 64

It's Okay to be Selfish! 66

Learn The Art of Mindful Loving 67

Show Love Multiple Times in Many Ways......................... 69

Learn The Signs Your Beloved Gives You ....

Dance The Masculine and Feminine Energy...................

Have You Found the Perfect Partner and Attained the Ultimate Love?...

About the Author ....

POSITIVELY DIVINE AND BEAUTIFULLY ABUNDANT... A RECIPE FOR LIFE ....

VALERIE SORRENTINO 81

About the Author ....1(

I M POSSIBLE...

ANGIE TOH 105

Introduction... 1(

When "Not Good Enough" is Your Mantra .... 1(

The Hysterectomy... 1(

Manifesting Miracles.. 1.

The Freak Fall .... 1.

Do Not Give Your Power Away.................................. 1.

Believe in the Possibilities.. 1.

Miracles Can Happen to Anyone .... 1.

Be Clear About What You Want to Manifest .... 1.

Maintain an Attitude of Gratitude .... 1.

Endings and Beginnings... 1.

About the Author .... 1.

THE POWER OF PRAYER, SELF-LOVE, AND INTENTION... THE KEYS TO MANIFESTING AND CREATING MIRACLES IN YOUR LIFE **127**

JACQUELINE VAN CAMPEN 127

Awareness Awakens our Senses to Be Present with Life 128

My Story 129

Encountering the Buddha Within 130

An Encounter with Love 134

After The Happily Ever After 134

Everything Begins with Intention 135

Enjoying the Gift of Manifestation 138

Letting Go of Judgment 141

How Does One Pray? 143

About the Author 145

MOMENTUM THROUGH MANIFESTING AND MIRACLES **147**

ANNA WEBER 147

The Four Dimensions of Manifestation 150

Desire 154

Direction 159

Determination 161

Discipline 164

Recognizing Miracles in the Midst of Frustration 165

The Necessity of Self-Reward 168

The Power of Strategic Planning.. 1(

Cherish... .... 1.

About the Author .... 1.

CONTRIBUTORS LISTING 175

Introduction

MIRACLES HAPPEN ALL the time and as mysterious as it seems, there are natural occurrences when we open ourselves to receiving and seeing from a different perspective. As I sat to write this book, it was a labor of love and clarion call of sorts—to let others know about creating a new life in a new and effortless manner. Sounds hokey, aye? Well, perhaps, but it is some wisdom is gleaned from this topic and the very nature of every story captured here.

Writing this sacred story was so heartfelt and transparent, that it made me question sharing such an intimate experience. However, I knew that in and of itself, the experience meant that I should forge ahead. Additionally, I know the co-authors encountered the same level of questioning at times. By no means are we perfect or live a perfect live, however, we've perfectly decided to take our lemons and make miraculous lemonade over and over and over again.

Now, you get to do the same thing with these eye-opening stories. May you deeply relate to these experiences; may you see your miraculous life contained within, and may you find—you.

Turn the page... Miracles, Momentum and Manifestation await you.

xoxo
Antoinette

Chapter 1

UNLEASE THE SECRET POWERS TO HAVING THE LIFE YOU DESIRE

Antoinette Sykes

Be still and know that I'm God.

~Psalm 46:10

WHERE DO YOU go to unleash the secret powers to having the life you desire? Upon what do you draw to connect with your belief in miracles... momentum... and manifestation?

In our uniqueness, we each find our own path to being super naturally ourselves, just as I find my own in nature and an ever-growing relationship with my creator. I hope to inspire you in sharing the pathway I walk to unleash my power, in the expectation that should you still be **seeking**... one of these experiences may motivate and direct you.

Looking into nature or simply being in nature seems to bring me to a place of a special **knowing** and a **sense** of sacred awareness. Everything seems to stand still... I can clearly hear the birds chirping, the squirrel nibbling and the water moving, and with that stillness is a miracle percolating. The miracle becomes the heightened

1

consciousness of what I see and hear, as well as the unseen; it is my taking time to pray and recognize there's something greater to every challenge that I face. In this stillness I come home, I come back to myself; and embrace once again that I am full of potential, wisdom and a surety that all is well with me, my current situation and life in general. While I don't know all the specific answers, the one answer I require appears before me... as needed—as each miracle unfolds.

Can You Relate?

MIRACLES ARE AVAILABLE to each of us of at any given time... if you openly and courageously surrender to your unchangeable *being* and choose to see things differently. This *seeing* is now through a different lens and from a complete and positive self-perspective, with a deep knowing that you are more than flesh—as we all are.

Stop and think for a moment of someone you have seen recently who perhaps did not deal well with life's challenges; someone you might sub-consciously have referred to as Debby Downer as you were jostled about in the midst of her negative spirit. Do you remember being aware of her being quite fearful... deep in her core and all that fear was coming to the surface various forms? Did you consider whether... if she was given another way to be, or see... she would?Is it possible you could have been the one to show her a better way to respond to those challenges as you sought to at least show her compassion? How would her day—and yours—have been transformed if you had chosen to send her love and blessings for the day?

Perhaps the bigger question remains... can you recall a time when **you** wore the Debby Downer title ... Fearful Franny... or Loveless Louise? Hopefully someone showed you a new way, showed compassion, and simply loved on you a little bit to help the cloud lift—enabling you to see another way—a peaceful loving way.

Miracles come at any time and they do not discriminate. To keep the momentum, there are certainly steps to keeping your awareness connected. In doing so, you begin to manifest, peace, love, joy, abundance and other limitless happiness—*all the time.*

Unleashing the power of being able to relate to others around you and being aware of the potential miracles available to you will reveal to you the secrets in life you've desired. And guess what? The biggest "secret" is that you already have the power within; you need only to connect to it and utilize it. For now, however, whenever you're facing a challenge and seem to have no answer, take a stroll in nature and simply become open to the answer availing to you. Ah... it really is that simple.

Supernaturally You...

AHEM! DID YOU know that you and I are spirit beings having a human experience? Have you ever sensed there was more... to you, to life, to your daily walk? I know I have. In fact, I revel in it. This deeper understanding seems to keep me centered and full of faith that no matter what happens—all things are in order—and working for my good. Doesn't it feel good just knowing that little truth?

3

In writing this story, I want you to experience the Spirit essence of you. So, tune in and listen to a sacred message I am confident I have heard from my Creator—on a spiritual level—that provides me all that I require when I need a reminder... a gentle nudging about how to reconnect with the power of miracles, and gain the momentum necessary to experience the manifestation of those things which most enrich my life. It is a conversation with my Creator; listen with me, if you will.

Dear Angel—before you were formed in your mother's womb, I knew you. I knew you'd be tall, friendly, with green eyes, and have a still, contemplative nature and certain innocence to you... even throughout your adult life. I knew you'd be extremely hopeful throughout your life, filled with the capacity to deeply feel love for others and crave the same kind of intimacy returned to you. I knew you'd have a **big personality***... one that fills the room with incredible light, energy and love. People would be drawn to you and you would think it's just a natural occurrence that happens for everyone. Well, my child, it doesn't. Granted, each of my children is filled with light, which shines for them the way it is supposed to.*

Oh, if only you would stop comparing your light to others. Light simply shines and there is no need for comparison; comparison is futile.

Through the early years, I watched you scrape your knee, curl your hair, succeed at schoolwork and be a happy child. You didn't know how much your spirit oozed from deep within you and at times, it was misunderstood. Others wanted to contain you in a box, when in fact, they were primarily responding to their pain and insecurity, and you *felt it; I saw it. I wanted you to reach out to me. Sometimes you did, but at other times you simply **took on** their abusive words. Why my child? Ah... you didn't think you were good enough because you looked different. I know. I know. Being the tallest kid in the classroom and being happy go lucky and being quite cute definitely had its challenges. But my child, you must know that kids will be kids. And all of those interactions actually served to push you closer to me.*

Angel—Oh, how your family showered you with love, fun and discipline. You learned this early on and it lifted you to become the woman you are today. With five protective uncles, a sassy aunt and her loving strong husband (like a surrogate dad), a doting grandmother and a loving lioness as a mother— you were bound for success. You see, they saw it early on, even when they didn't see it in themselves. They saw it for you—in you—and only wanted to push you to be the best. Now, that's love, dear. Oh, and while we're focusing on family—it is important you know your dad loved and loves you, sweetie. He just chose not to be in your life. But that had nothing—I repeat—nothing to do with you. You were and still are simply beautiful and strong and loving. You deserve all the good things coming your way.

Angel—Oh, how the formative years shaped your view of yourself. As we talk about miracles, the one lesson for you and others is to know that you are never alone. Yes, life can have lonely moments, but you are never alone. That's not how I designed you or my kingdom. Be still. Shhh... you feel that? That peace? That's me. Now, today, I know you have come to know that truth. In fact, I love how you love to spend time with me. I love you. Dry your tears and simply heal. You are free.

The Natural Way of Miracles

EVEN THOUGH YOU have the capacity to be supernatural, understand your miracles are natural occurrences. That's the message of this book. Each miracle is a natural occurrence because as a spirit being, miracles are a natural way of being. It may seem supernatural or sudden, but the only thing sudden is your remembrance of the spirit-being qualities that you already possess. Everyone does, but so few understand the process of tapping into them. So, how does one tune into these miracles and keep the momentum of manifesting the desires of life?

1. Simply believe...

2. Pray and move your feet always in a direction toward love...
3. Walk in faith...

4. Expect to receive as you've prayed...

5. Give thanks—no matter what things look like to the naked eye...

6. Share your light—brightly and boldly...

7. Be still and spend time with me...

8. Dream big and then dream bigger...

9. Have fun, laugh and love...

10. Love with your whole heart—it will be returned to you 100 times over...

11. Repeat one through ten.

How did I come to know these things? Let's return to another conversation with my Creator...

*Today, I'm proud of you. You've come through lots of transition and pain and tears. You know that I've been with you. Now, my dear, it's time that you let the past go. Really let it go. Sometimes we hang onto the past... much like our favorite garments. I mean for you to step out of those layers of "clothes" that have weighed you down. I know, I know, you've said you've let it go. And some of it you have...but **not** all of it. **Now** is the time to let it all go. **You must...** in order to see all of the miracles fulfilled and your prayers answered. It's ok. Forget it.*

*I'm doing something new and lovely—with just your name on it. But, here is where you get to trust and surrender to your True spirit essence. It's time. I see your dreams, desires, tears and wants. **Now** is the time to release all that does not serve you and step out of those old garments. There are new clothes for you to stroll into a miraculous future— filled with your heart's desires.*

Angel—Are you ready to release it... the past? I think you are. I know, I know. It's scary. But also know that I didn't give you a spirit of fear—to cripple you. No! That is nothing more than your cunning ego wanting to keep you safe, dear. Trust me. You're safe. So, if you're ready... what you want is on the other side of whatever fear prevents your releasing the past.

One last thing, when you release those things that no longer serve you, be sure to never return "there" again. Use the lessons you have learned to help you make better future decisions, but don't pick up the pain and story filled with

7

fear – ever again. It's not suited for where you're going... your future is brighter than your past.

I stand in my quiet contemplation...

Are you ready?

A tearful, "Yes!"

Good, then repeat this: Today I release all of my tears, fears and unbelief about who I was. I release the blame I held towards others and the blame against myself. I release the shame of past decisions and actions. I release the disappointments in life. They no longer serve me and I gladly shed each of those garments of fear, shame, guilt and sabotage. In this moment, I bless my past and send it with healing and thanksgiving for pushing me to all that lies before me.

Now, with all my miraculous God-given power, I now step into my bright future – secure in finding for fervent fruit and love. So it is. Miracles abound... manifestations of my prayers are in the midst. I receive them today and today extends into the future.

Ah... now that's momentum...

Amen!

Angel...

ANGEL IS MY nickname. So when He speaks, He speaks to me on that level—very personally. It's important to know that you too can have this communication with God—in fact, you do. But, often we're not still enough to listen. I simply ask you to speak to Him from your heart. I promise, He will speak back with treasures only you know to be true and which are made just for you. As you settle in to read the other stories, walk in this **divine knowing** that you are where you are supposed to be... in order to experience your next miracle.

About the Author

TRANSFORMATION LIFE COACH Antoinette Sykes, helps others transform, transition and triumphantly live the life they've only imagined -of freedom and unlimited happiness, with a fervent belief that you can live the life you truly dream of and not settle if you trust all things are possible through the one that created you.

As {An} Unsinkable Soul, Antoinette uses the knowledge derived from a BS in Psychology, MBA in Marketing, and a Subconscious Reconditioning Life Coaching certification—combined with life experiences as an elite workplace leader, survivor of two layoffs, and losing her fiancé to suicide—to smilingly help others transform, transition and triumphantly live the life of freedom and unlimited happiness they've only imagined.

At any given time you can find Antoinette, who is a lover of life and all things self-help, living to her image of being ridiculously happy... inspiring the masses via speaking, social media or one of her coaching programs, and singing with her hairbrush as the microphone!

http://AntoinetteSykes.com
antoinette@antoinettesykes.com
http://www.amazon.com/Antoinette-Sykes/e/B00CPRL0CS
https://twitter.com/AntoinetteSykes

Chapter 2

LEARNING TO LISTEN

Amber J. Boswell

"The only limitations in life are self-imposed"

~Amber J. Boswell

MIRACLES, MOMENTUM AND Manifesting… it took me many years to understand that once we begin to consciously design the life we desire, we have the ability to manifest miracles, creating a momentum that can literally transform every aspect of our lives. My journey to this place of deep empowering realization was a long, treacherous one filled with many trials and tribulations. However, I believe it is through adversity we truly discover who we are. I also believe that strength is birthed through authentic vulnerability. In order to achieve true enlightenment we must be willing to get naked with ourselves, we must be willing to truly look at ourselves both literally and metaphorically; to be able to hold our own gaze in the mirror regardless of how scary that may seem. Once we have had that intimate exchange between how we perceive ourselves, and the true essence of who we are, it can be difficult to accept ourselves, for we are not defined by our past. I could have easily chosen the path of the Victim with all that has "happened to me," but I *choose* to be the Victor, and it is through my choice to stand up and share my story that I am setting the intention that somewhere out there one of you will read it and realize *you* don't have to settle for anything less than the life you were divinely designed to live.

My Story

THROUGH MY WINE induced haze I saw his brown eyes turn black and glaze over, his left eye sagging and I knew he had flipped the switch, he was blacked out again.

"Fucking whore, fat Bitch, Cunt."

His usual verbal daggers came flying toward me, however I had grown numb to his attacks; after 13 years of abuse and the reliable comfort I found in the bottom of a bottle, his words no longer hurt me. He had become increasingly aware of the control he was losing over me; even in his drunken rage he was able to read my indifference, this awakened the angry demons dwelling within him. My suffering, once the antidote for the pain and shame he has carried around his whole existence had diminished, fueling his rage.

I ignored him, turning to my sister to continue our conversation.

"You're worthless, you good for nothing slut."

12

He continued until I had reached my capacity for his battering, and replied, "Leave me alone, I hate you." While this was certainly not a mature response, it was the one he was looking to invoke.

This was all he needed, what he was poking and prodding me for... a response. He grabbed the knife on the kitchen counter used earlier in the preparation of dinner for our two small children. He lunged toward me stopping at my stomach saying, " I will kill you, you bitch."

His eyes were the darkest and most evil I had ever seen. His brother grabbed him—my sister me. Interesting how he often compared our love story to Sid and Nancy. You may recall the story of Sid Vicous, the star of the 80's punk band Sex Pistols, whose toxic-love turned-tragic when through a drug induced haze Sid stabbed and killed Nancy. Ironically, he had used this comparison about our own toxic relationship for years, as the pair was dangerously co-dependent on one another and now, always attempting to reenact their ending.

This was a far cry from the Cinderella Story I had envisioned for my life. In that moment, that awful, terrifying moment I made the decision *not* to live in fear anymore, *not* to allow my daughters to grow up witness to their mother's abuse, or worse, her weakness. I *did not* have to suffer anymore.

The next morning I woke up... hung over from the wine and the 13 years I had spent with the man I thought would love, honor, and protect me, yet turned out to be the man that would steal my innocence, strip me of my strength, yet also give me the greatest gifts I have ever received, my daughters Kaya and Kaylyn—and in the end—myself!

Where Does It Begin?

MY MEMORIES OF life don't extend back much further than age four. There is video footage somewhere amongst the hundreds of boxes in my mother's garage of my pre-school graduation where we are all on stage accepting our diplomas. I recall when asked what we wanted to be when we grew up... mine was not among the common answers most gave when each small child came forth: doctor, lawyer, firemen, and police officer. Oh, no! When it came to me, I very matter of factly stated: "Princess." I share this not because I wanted to be a princess, but because as a young child I innately I knew I was entitled to any life I desired.

I also remember daydreaming of my prince charming; he was a cross between the Prince in Cinderella and Prince Eric from the Little Mermaid. I couldn't wait to grow up and fall in love. However, my view on love became tainted from a young age when I walked into my Mother and Father's restaurant, and witnessed tears streaming down my Dad's face. In my little mind, my Dad was—in my world—the strongest man alive. I looked at him and then at my Mother who was looking down; being quite the intuitive child, I immediately postured, "You're getting a divorce!"

Unfortunately, that divorce spelled for me a long and winding road of living in different places and spaces with different people; the only "home" I ever knew was my family's vacation cabin nestled at the end of a

14

private road overlooking the Tule River... anyone who has a cabin up there will confirm it is the best place on earth.

My mother, to whom I am now very close, chose the divorce. Now, as a mother of three, I understand her reasoning, which I don't need to disclose here. That was her journey and this is mine. At the time, however, I interpreted her choice to leave my father as choosing to leave my little sister, and me, and since I chose to remain with my father, my little four-year old sister chose to stay with me. Our father suddenly became a single dad to two girls.

We lived on a Yacht in the Cabrillo Yacht Club Harbor in San Pedro, California; the only thing my father really got to keep in the divorce. This was a magical time for my sister and I as we anchored in Catalina every other weekend. Next to the cabin, Catalina became our one constant... if not on the water, we were in it, and the Pacific Ocean became my first love. I would lie awake at night waiting to hear my dad's snore grumbling from under his cabin door and climb out of the window above my bed onto the bow of the boat. Often my sister would climb out of her window and meet me there breathing in the salt air, allowing the boat to dance gracefully in its dock staring at the stars that were like thousands of diamonds, counting on them to mesmerize us as we talked about life. We allowed our selves to dream... again; I dreamt of my prince.

As life would have it, I soon realized my father was a ladies man who ended up having a long string of girlfriends and wives, none of which I was fond. The one he married when I was nine did not like the relationship my father and I shared—somehow sensing that our bond was unbreakable. Being born on the same day, she must have assumed we were "cut from the same cloth."

To this day my father remains my best friend. Unfortunately, our relationship threatened the woman I nicknamed to my sister as Cruella Deville. She was a mean spirited woman to begin with, but her disdain for me grew by the day. She had two daughters; the youngest my age. During one of our typical childhood spats, who should walk in but Cruella, who grabbed and held me down while her daughter repeatedly kicked me. Sometimes, life *is fair* and shields children with a protective blanket... my father walked in and we left that night, this was the day I swore I would never marry!

Life's Lessons Follow Us...

FAST FORWARD A few years... my sister and I had grown older and inevitably more challenging. As a single working father my Dad craved a break, which led to me spending a month out of each summer with my Grandmother—whom I affectionately called MiMi—in our family's summer home, "The Cabin." From a very early age MiMi had assumed the maternal role in my life; the time I spent there was filled with learning from MiMi how to be a woman, or in her words, "A lady." She taught me how to cook, how to properly set a table, which fork to use, and which glass to drink from. Her famous saying was "You need to know how to dine with the Queen," MiMi also taught me countless other lessons in life: how to be frugal yet still enjoy the finer things in life, how to play cards like a shark, how to take care of my blossoming body, most

16

specifically to take are of my "hair and skin because you only get one set." However, her biggest lesson, which I only now understand as a mother and a wife, included that of how to be a matriarch.

When not in MiMi Training, I was free to roam the mountain, hike barefoot, swim naked in the river, learn the native berries and plants, and what I could and couldn't eat if I valued my life. I connected with my inner self and the earth there... I still do. It was during those summers I started to realize there was something bigger out there, and it was through nature I started to see the magic in life.

However, as time went on my father desired more personal time, which resulted in him sending us more frequently to our Mother's. I fought tooth and nail as I hated where she lived, and unfortunately during those tween years, even felt I hated her. On one of our visits I went to her best friend's house; she just happened to have a daughter a year older than I was. We found our moms off somewhere, and decided to have a party of our own with her boyfriend who was 17 and his friend who was 18. We were 12 and 13 with bodies of 16 year olds—the boys brought tequila; we brought our naivety.

I found myself in a room alone with the older one; he reeked of alcohol and started to kiss me. I had never really kissed a boy before; the whole experience was uncomfortable and awkward. Eventually, he began to tug at my clothes; my voice getting caught in my throat as I wiggled underneath his firm grasp and his 200-pound frame. Of course, he wouldn't stop until he reached his desired destination... in the natural ways of life, I let out a huge scream, he cupped my mouth, I bit him, and screamed again. He was taken aback as I flew for the door, and although I escaped, I was naked from the waist down, my shirt ripped, my face stained with mascara I shouldn't have been wearing, and my childhood—lost.

Finding Beauty in the Dimmed Light of Shattered Dreams

FROM THAT POINT forward I disregarded my fantasies of true love, succumbing to the belief that Prince Charming, if he did indeed exist, was surely not coming for me... I was damaged goods. I became wild and out of control, which resulted in my being sent to a group home, which I manipulated my way out of, and then to my grandparents for more than just a summer visit. Needless to say, I ran away and my shattered dreams wound up breaking MiMi's heart—the one person who believed in and lovingly tried to help raise me. If I were called upon to fit the years between 12-15 in a separate memoir, it would be titled, *Lucky to Be Alive!*

My dreams continued to become my greatest disillusionments. At age 15 I was sent to live with my mother, who had since moved on from her life with my father, and in with my brother's father on the Tule River Indian Reservation. I went from waking up, walking out my front door, barefoot down to the beach, to waking up to a cow in my window in the middle of nowhere—in a tiny shack of a house with a wood stove for heat, and plywood for flooring. To this day I swear that house was haunted...

There must be some beauty even in the dimmed lights of shattered dreams; mine was finding how much I loved living with my baby brother, and the joy I found pretending he was mine. At first I tried to embrace this new, yet odd cowboy lifestyle. I befriended a wolf that would never come too close, but always followed me to the river—almost as if he was watching over me. I would sunbathe nude, write in my journals, and get lost in books. It was a foreign way of life. As my memory travels back to that time, I remember being asked to describe my mother and father and my response was, "It is something like Country meets Country Club."

It all makes perfect sense—now—why they couldn't exist in one another's world... leaving me to feel as if I didn't fit in anywhere! The kids at school called me Malibu Barbie, White Rich Snob, White Bitch... oh, the list was endless! One momentous night I heard a screech outside of my bedroom window I quickly looked at the clock. It was 2:00 AM. Despite the hour, I seemed compelled to pull back the sheet that was my curtain, and through the infamous Tule Fog I could make out headlights of a car that had crashed through our fence. Instantly I was panicked, I grabbed the phone and ran out toward them offering my help in case someone was hurt, only to bear the brunt of abuse by a young Indian driver who was visibly intoxicated. Imagine my repulsion as he stumbled from his car and looking at me through the narrow, blood-red-slits of his eyes and slurred, "I don't need anything from you white bitch!" The arrogance followed as he pulled out his penis and proceeded to urinate—yelling, "This is what I think of you, get off our land, white bitch!"

19

Terrified, I didn't know how to respond other than to wake up my mother; she called my brother's uncle who came out to greet him with a shotgun. In that instant, I reviewed the reality of the scene and decided I had absolutely no desire to live in the Wild-Wild West, and from that point forward I would find every excuse possible to sleep down the hill at my step sister's house... away from what I perceived as madness, only to find more madness.

Not much good can come from being a confused 15-year old girl, with the body of 19 year old, who lies about her age. The lack of maturity was well exhibited one night at a party where I met a drunk and obnoxious older man who felt compelled make nasty comments to me as he chased me around his house riding a broom as if it was a toy horse. I should have known in that moment he would be bad for me, but as fate would have it his house was "the" party house; it was where we would all go to drink ourselves stupid, play poker, barbecue, and pass time. His house became my refuge.

He was 30; I was 15. My life would forever be changed because this person—also from Orange County—had also grown up skating, surfing, and snowboarding, and was the first person in that crazy place I felt trapped in I felt even came close to understanding me. We became friends and the anxious events of the first night we met faded. We went wake boarding, camping, and listened to alternative music instead of the ghetto rap or mariachi music that you'd normally hear blasting on the streets. In retrospect, I sense he was the closest thing to "home" I could find in this new "hell" and I suppose some part of me labeled him as my hero... my savior.

I knew he was too old, but I didn't care; I rather liked it—truth be told. I allowed myself to "fall in love" for the first time, and for the first time in a long time, I felt safe. It wasn't long after my father discovered what was going on that he finally brought me home to Orange County and I was free to be me again. I had tried to move on, dating what was "cool" as a teenage girl: pro-surfers, body boarders, snowboarders, motocross riders, but I still convinced myself I missed the guy I thought saved me. My junior year he came down to visit me during Christmas break; we drove around Laguna Beach taking in the Ocean, breathing in one another, sober yet drunk with lust. It was there we pulled over on the side of the Pacific Coast Highway, and our daughter Kaya, the child I believe saved and shifted my life, was conceived.

Someday, I will write an actual memoir and go more into detail about the wildness of my life, but I am sure it is obvious that I made many immature and reckless decisions as a young girl. I often wonder about what my life would look like had Kaya not been born, if I would even be alive to write this. I believe Kaya was the first real miracle in my life, by being blessed with a child of my own I was forced to "grow up" and began to take my life more seriously, I am forever grateful for her.

I found myself 16 and Pregnant! I was scared, I was ashamed, I was thrilled, and we were scheduled to get married, but I soon found out I was not the only one expecting a baby by him. I called off the wedding and he abandoned me during the pregnancy, leaving my father to hold my hand through the whole process. Some eight months later, after a two-day vacation in Las Vegas County Jail, he decided he wanted to help raise our daughter. I was probably swayed by the fact he was there for the birth, so at a mere 17 years of age, I moved in with my 32-year old boyfriend, his 8-year old daughter, and my newborn baby. In a way Shawn helped raise me, shaping me to be what he desired; again not the fairytale I had long imagined, I found I was losing more control to him with each passing year.

I was young and ever hopeful and there were times where we were happy; times where for the first time since I was six I felt like I was part of a family. At 19 I was pregnant again with our second daughter, Kaylyn, who breathed life back into me—and us—for a time. However, as time went on, he began to drink more and more, and became increasingly jealous and paranoid, which led to many violent outbursts. One night after attending night class at the local community college I entered the house, it was dark, I was greeted by being slammed against the wall and strangled until I passed out. This is when I left for the first time, beginning years of a back-and-forth relationship. We were on, off, on and off; the days filled with abuse, infidelity, and alcoholism... years of living together, years of living apart.

Finally, I thought I had overcome my past, and there was a three year stint where I had moved on in a different relationship, ran a real estate and mortgage company with my father, and had a beautiful 2,500 square foot home overlooking the golf course and ocean in San Clemente, California. I drove a Lexus, my kids were attending private school, and I thought I had it all. Then I was humbled. I did not anticipate the Real Estate crash of 2007 and in one month, lost my boyfriend, my house, my business, and my car. Guess who was there to pick up the pieces? We were always connected; we were one another's vice.

For a moment there was love, but again with the passing of time, the shadows of the past reemerged and the relationship became so toxic it would have killed one of us, and on that day in the spring of 2010 I decided it sure as hell wouldn't be me. I'd had enough!

Adding Momentum to Manifesting Dreams

I WAS 28; I wasn't a girl anymore and had girls of my own for whom I was responsible. What was I teaching them? Who was I showing them to be? It sure as hell wasn't the strong matriarch my Grandmother taught me to be, and I knew deep in my heart if she were around to witness my choices it would have destroyed her. I called my grandfather, asking him if I could go to our "cabin" to get my head on straight and devise a plan of escape and liberation.

At the time I owned a Mercedes Benz, the same age as I was. It had an awful turquoise paint job faded from beach living, a window that wouldn't roll up, so if it rained the kids and I were wet, and a transmission that never could have made it up the mountain. I took the last bit of money from my bank account—and the cash I had hidden in an old pillowcase—and had my friend drive me up there.

I remembered having what many refer to as a "spiritual awakening" two years prior at a Goddess retreat where I was reintroduced to my higher self; my soul. It was one of the most beautiful and memorable weekends of my life. It was unlike anything I had ever experienced and even though I was born in the 80's, I lived like I was in the 60's for a time and I can attest no drug compares to the euphoria of connecting to the Divine. I came back from that retreat wide-awake and unable to go back to sleep. I was so excited, I thought "OMG It has finally happened, I am finally enlightened!" "Now my life will all fall into place" Ha! The Universal joke was on me! This was simply the beginning of what I now know and accept as a life long journey! Every one has their own individual journey and in most life stories we all come to the cliché we call the "fork in the road" and this was mine... I just had no idea which way to turn, so I paused and went to the one place that I knew would provide the answer.

I had my sister take my girls, knowing this needed to be a solo mission; I needed to seek the counsel of the soul-self I had met two years prior in that room full of women I didn't know, who were courageously chanting and "marrying" themselves at a retreat in the Heart of Orange County. I needed to know where that excited and inspired woman had been hiding over the past two years, while I was living heavily immersed in duality. Walking a spiritual path to enlightenment during the day and in a world of darkness come nightfall. Where was she?

The first few days I spent my time in silence, walking the forest, watching movies on satellite, eating any comfort food I could find to avoid the bottle, and the meeting I had with the Universe... until one day I got up the courage to walk up to the clearing above our cabin that ironically Shawn had cleared as a spot to honor my grandmother's memory. I sat on the benches my grandfather had placed there and said aloud, "Ok, God, Goddess, Universe, MiMi... I surrender! I don't desire to live like this anymore; tell me what to do!" I then took out the journal my eldest daughter had given to me prior to my trip and began to write as if it was one year later. I had heard about doing this type of intentional writing to assist in manifesting the life you desire, but had never tried it. At this point I was broken... emotionally, spiritually, and mentally depleted and willing to do anything to change my life.

I did not hold back; I wrote out all I desired to create—a new reality—including the fantasy of true love I held onto as a little girl. I decided I would bury my writing in the ground under the tree where we had placed my grandmother's ashes seven years prior. As I began to dig up the dirt, a metal pendant came up out of the ground; it was old, purple, and had two birds on the front. I turned it over and the name Laurel Burch was on the back. I didn't know what to make of this, who this Laurel Burch was, and why her neck was anywhere near my grandmother's tree! I ran down to the cabin and immediately called my Dad; he had never heard the name, nor had my grandfather or my sister. Confused, I skimmed the directory searching for her name, and came away with nothing! We don't have Internet in a place that relishes being disconnected from the world yet connected to earth and family.

I called my friend, Abra, and had her Google the name and sure enough, Laurel Burch turned out to be a famous artist whose life mirrored mine in many ways. She was a troubled teen who had ran away from her Orange County home at age 14, and started making jewelry from things she would find on the street. Over time, Laurel grew her "brand" and was able to support the two children she had given birth to by age 20. She also went on to become a spiritual speaker, which is my own ultimate dream.

Listening for the Miracles

NEEDLESS TO SAY, my head was spinning with the miracle of this poignant sign that literally came out of nowhere; I decided to take a walk on the trails behind our cabin. What followed was a lot of talking to God and my soul-self. There was a lot of inner dialogue—mostly addressing it was time to leave the toxic relationship and toxic living behind me. Then, like a scene straight from the big screen I heard a voice say, "Move here in the month of July."

I froze and then whispered, "How am I suppose to do that? I don't have enough money to move to the mountains."

"You must listen in order to have what you desire!" The strange voice grew louder "Move here in July!"

Perplexed by what felt like I had just entered into a different dimension, I continued to walk in silence until I came upon three doe, not deer, doe...three females, another sign that there were three of us involved in this decision

"Move here in July!" Again the voice boomed, echoing through the mountains... the doe unaffected as they stood there staring at me. Anyone who has spent time in the mountains knows this is very unusual, as deer/doe usually run away at the first site of a human. My eyes locked with what appeared to be the mother, "You must trust the Universe in order to manifest," the voice said in a nurturing tone.

"If I am really supposed to just up and move here when I take a step, you'll remain there," I challenged the doe and the Universe.

They stood firm. "Ok, I will do it, I will move here in July." Following that commitment, the doe scattered up the hill.

I practically ran to the cabin, dug out an old Jack Daniels Box to place my writings in and ran back to MiMi's spot to bury my manifestation in the earth. I opened the journal Kaya had gifted me prior to me going up the mountain; on the inside flap was written "Laurel Burch 1999, Self Portrait." As an artist Laurel had created a journal line as well. Mind racing... *What are the odds? How could this really be?*

The Journal was never near this spot before and until this day I had never heard of this woman who seemed to be speaking to me. I fell to ground and began to sob. *How can this be?*

"You asked for an answer, you have one, now you must learn how to listen," the voice comforted me in my mystified, emotional, and grateful state.

Five days later my sister brought up my girls and my entire family joined us for our annual Memorial Day weekend family retreat. The cabin community consists of 50 privately owned cabins where each generation has grown up together—one generation of kids after another. In fact, my grandfather first visited his uncle there when he was just four. It is the only place I had ever truly "grown-up" knowing the same people year after year. One of the friends we grew up with came to call on my sister; she was in bed so I invited him to share a glass of wine on the deck.

He said, "I am more of a Jack Daniels man, but sure."

A vision of the card box flashed in my mind; I brushed it off. We shared a glass of Pinot Noir and years of stories until two AM; it was nice to connect with someone from my youth. He had just moved to Corcoran to fulfill his own life long dream and planned on visiting the cabin in the summer to escape the heat of the Valley floor. I shared my crazy story and how I would be living there in July, we agreed to keep in touch and hang out during the summer.

June all to quickly came and went; the very day the girls were out of school I packed our belongings, emptied the money-laden pillowcase and made my blind voyage to the cabin—not once entertaining the idea of love, nor desiring it. My sister's old friend became my new one! Dan and I had dinner a few times, talking and keeping one another company. One night during our meal Dan was sharing with me how he had just taken on coaching a peewee football team on the side. I was suddenly very aware of a white light shining all around him, and in that moment I knew he was the man I was going to marry. Dan must have felt the same emotions, because that night he kissed me.

We were married less than a year later on May 21, 2011... right above where I had buried my "manifestation" on May 26, 2010, in which I had written, "I am with the man I will marry, he accepts me for all that I am, he supports and encourages my spiritual growth, he loves my children, we have a child together."

Today, I am blessed to know Dan is all of those things and more. He is the Prince Charming I was looking for; little does it matter that instead of a showing up on a white horse, he showed up wearing a head lamp and smelling of bug spray. To say we are destined is an understatement; we have the same markings on our arm and have crossed one another's path since birth. In the end, I got my fairytale.

We just recently purchased our dream home in the Foothills of Los Angeles, California, we have a beautiful 21-month-old daughter, he loves my two older girls like his own, and above all he allows me to be me. However, if I had not listened to the voices in the forest that May day in 2010, I don't know where I would be—definitely not writing this book and maybe not even breathing. From that point forward I have learned to listen to the Universe (the voice), no matter how crazy it may seem. I urge you to learn how to identify the signs and listen to your own inner "voice" for you never know what miracles await you!

About the Author

AMBER J BOSWELL works with clients to co-create a custom life design that empowers them to not only live the life of their dreams, but also to step into their divine purpose and birthright of abundance.

From being raped, robbed at gun point, battling various addictions—one of which was love; from building a successful business to losing everything; and from being homeless to discovering her divine purpose and designing the life of her dreams... Amber has personally walked through the fires of life and risen from the ashes as the Phoenix she is. She believes that our greatest gifts lie in our greatest challenges and if we were willing to use those experiences to empower us rather then hinder us, the world would surely be a better place.

It is **this woman** Amber has become, through embracing the possibilities of miracles, adding personal responsibilities to fuel the momentum of life changes, and reaping the rewards of manifesting her deepest desires. Today, she fervently believes every person on the planet has the ability to design the lives to which they are divinely entitled, working from the premise that desire and determination define the individual –not their circumstances. She does not come with a long list of credentials following her name, or a long chain of diplomas hanging on an office wall. What she offers is endless life experiences of potential defeat... to which she responds with the Chinese Proverb, "Get knocked down seven times and get back up eight."

Connect with Amber at...

www.linkedin.com/pub/amber-boswell/85/5aa/8ba
https://www.facebook.com/amber.boswell.562

Chapter 3

BREAKDOWN TO BREAKTHROUGH
Mary Canty Merrill, Ph.D.

"Every challenge that we face is a fork in the road that beckons us left, right, backward or forward. Yet sometimes, our journey has rendered us paralyzed and we must breakdown to breakthrough."

– Mary Canty Merrill, PhD

Introduction

THE EXTRAORDINARY TITLE, *Miracles, Momentum and Manifestation*, caught my attention before I ever knew about its planned contents, which is why I was so enthusiastic about participating in this project. Early on, I sat down with these three words to ponder their deepest meaning and as a result, made some amazing discoveries about life in general and myself in particular.

When I was initially asked to share a life-changing story in this book, I wondered what story I could possibly share that would even remotely inspire another. The answer came, but because of fear and shame, I was not quick to embrace it. In fact, I vehemently resisted it. However, I ultimately discovered that when something is important to our soul's evolution, we can expect to feel a significant amount of resistance and discomfort. This point will gain clarity as you read my story.

In the meantime, let me share with you what miracles, momentum and manifestation mean to me. When I think of **miracles**, I think of improbable events that defy the laws of science and nature. They surpass all human logic because they occur through Divine intervention. In reflecting on **momentum**, I think of gaining strength and forward movement that compels and propels me to higher ground. **Manifestation** is the physical evidence of the seeds that I have planted and the things that I have hoped for. It is a public display of my testimony signaling that I have arrived in a new and different place.

Sometimes, we must live the questions in order to receive the answers. Of the many challenges that I have faced in life, the earliest and most difficult to navigate was debilitating depression. For obvious reasons, this is not something that I have publicized, so very few people are even aware I suffer from the condition. Nonetheless, despite numerous trials and tribulations that I have encountered as a result of depression, I am a walking testament that miracles do exist.

I know this because the Universe (God, for me) had to break me down early in life to bring me to the place where I can boldly follow the path that He has designed. As miracles manifest in my life, I am grateful for his design.

For years, I nursed a spirit of anxiety-ridden perfection, which I liken to stumbling around in the dark without a flashlight, never knowing when you will trip and fall or how damaging that fall will be. I was more concerned with my outward appearance than I was with my internal condition. My external shell was superficial (at best) but beneath the surface, I was a train wreck waiting to happen.

Because I was living a double life, I avoided allowing anyone to get too close, lest they discover that I was not the perfect person that I so confidently portrayed. Yet, fifty-one years and life experiences have taught me that no one or nothing is perfect. There is a crack in everything, which is how the light is able to penetrate and illuminate darkness. In striving for perfection, we spend an inordinate amount of valuable time and unnecessary energy trying to sustain a façade... while missing the essence and the blessing of who we really are.

Life is a pilgrimage of discovery that takes us on a journey from darkness into light. We cannot lead where we have never gone, so I am convinced it is vitally important to examine and understand that from which we came before we can fully and lovingly embrace who we are and appreciate the unique gifts that we have been blessed to offer.

In my persistent quest for authenticity, I am baring my soul in this chapter to give voice to a dark period in my life that shocked me, shook me, sharpened me, shaped me, and propelled me to this moment in time. I use this story as a platform to speak as I have never spoken before— from my heart, rather than my head. I do not share my story to elicit a sympathetic reaction. Nor do I have any intention other than to be a source of inspiration and a guiding light for those struggling with life's debilitating challenges and wondering how to take that first step towards overcoming them. I believe that the inspired soul can do anything, so nothing is impossible. If you are committed to climbing out of your well-worn rut and unleashing your own miracles, momentum and manifestation, this story is dedicated to you. Get still... let me tell you about my personal journey from hellish darkness into illuminating light.

The Back Story

THE FIRST TIME I actually remember experiencing depression was at the ripe old age of thirteen. Of course, at the time I did not know that I was depressed nor could I pinpoint any one incident that prompted my bouts of despair. However, decades later I now understand that my depression was not solely triggered by any external source, but also by an internal chemical imbalance that would plague me for a lifetime.

Until we face our inner demons, all roads will lead to pain and suffering. When we are walking around as an empty shell wearing a mask, we are destined for trouble. This depression took up residence and consumed me for many years before I ever acknowledged or addressed it. Despite my ignorance about depression, I suffered all the classic symptoms: anxiety, sadness, irritability, insomnia, difficulty concentrating and making decisions, decreased energy, and a loss of interest in activities that I once enjoyed.

Writing this story dredges up painful memories as if I experienced them only yesterday. The difference is that today, I have finally given myself permission to fully acknowledge and experience all of my feelings and emotions, regardless how painful they may be. Resilience and authenticity are the reasons why I am able to openly share this very private part of my life with you, and I will begin with the significance of feelings and emotions.

Repressed Feelings and Emotions

WHILE THE TERMS *feelings* and *emotions* are often used interchangeably, I believe there are distinct differences. *Feelings* are superficial and constructed by the reactions of our five senses – touch, taste, sight, sound and smell – to external stimuli. For example, depending upon the season when I go outside, I might feel hot, sweaty or cold. If I am going for a doctor's visit, I might feel anxious, nervous or scared.

Emotions are deep-seated and represent a state of consciousness that is associated with our interpretations and impressions of our experiences. Psychological research has identified five primary emotions that are similar across all cultures: love, hate, fear, joy and sorrow, which are our body's natural response to threats and opportunities, so it might help to think in terms of survival.

The biggest difference between feelings and emotions is that external forces trigger feelings, whereas emotions can be completely internalized. Feelings are experienced for short periods of time and end when the external triggering event has passed; emotions are long-term states which last for days, months, or even years. Because emotions are internal, in order to change them a shift in thoughts and beliefs must first occur.

I make these distinctions between feelings and emotions because in hindsight, I am now able to see that I had closed off the most significant aspects of myself. While repressing feelings and emotions can be healthy in terms of giving us sufficient time to work through them, they can also become overwhelming and physically harmful when allowed to go indefinitely unchecked. With my feelings and emotions buried, I was literally disconnected from painful thoughts and memories that needed to be addressed before I could move forward—or gain momentum. I also found it difficult to trust, so isolated myself by keeping everyone at a distance to avoid appearing vulnerable. Little did I know, I *was* in fact so vulnerable that I would eventually fold in on myself and ultimately collapse.

Repressing feelings and emotions is a regular strategy that many people use to cope with difficult situations. No one wants to walk around feeling miserable all of the time, yet when we repress our feelings and emotions, we become dominated by our unconscious mind and set ourselves up for more problems. Negative forces begin to build internally and broil beneath the surface. These powerful forces seep out in various ways and at inopportune times, until the pressure becomes so intense that the mind snaps and the body breaks down.

Psychotherapy

GROWING UP, I was taught that one should never air their dirty laundry in public. If and when they do, it is akin to breaking a sacred familial contract. I was also acutely aware of the social stigma that surrounded depression, especially in the African American community. As a result of these deeply ingrained beliefs, fear, guilt and burning shame, I was extremely reluctant to seek professional help in getting my life back on track. When I reached the point of incapacitation—being unable to fully function in normal daily activities—in my mid-20s, I knew that something had to change.

My first experience with a psychotherapist was not a good one. I can vividly recall sitting in his office one day sharing a traumatic experience while void of all the emotion that one would expect from an adjusted person, and he was taken aback. After several sessions, he concluded that he could not work with me, because I was extremely psychologically and emotionally guarded which made him feel very uncomfortable, making it difficult for him to penetrate the thick shell that I had so carefully constructed. I came to perceive this as rejection, which devastated me, and came daringly close to calling the whole psychotherapy thing quits before ever really getting started.

The good news is I did not give up and started working with a different therapist who met me where I was. She was competent, had a good reputation in the clinical community, did not pass judgment and allowed me to "unfold" in my own time and in my own way. As a result, I became more comfortable sharing my secrets, fears, hopes and aspirations. She gave her all in helping me to begin peeling back those seemingly impenetrable layers, work through some difficult issues, set personal boundaries and make more healthy decisions. I grew to love and trust this woman implicitly and she remains a dear friend and confidante to this day. (She and her new husband even traveled to attend my destination wedding festivities in 2004. How cool is that!)

A crucial turning point emerged in psychotherapy when I emphatically refused to take supplemental medications to help regulate my moods. I was still in deep denial and thought that depression was something I could easily overcome with just a few more therapy sessions. Unfortunately (or fortunately, depending upon how it is viewed), I was to soon discover that psychotherapy alone was no match for my persistent and severe condition.

Breakdown – Reduced to Ashes

IN GREEK MYTHOLOGY, the mystical Phoenix was a beautiful brightly colored bird with golden-red plumage that was said to be as large as an eagle and emit radiant light. This bird, known as the firebird of the sun, was believed to have a 500 to 1,000 year life cycle, and when it grew tired and reached the end of its life, it erupted into flames and was reduced to a pile of ashes. I have always been fascinated by the story of the Phoenix, so I use its death and resurrection as a metaphor for my own experience.

A *breakdown* is a sudden loss of ability to effectively function in day-to-day life. It is a mental collapse that occurs when life's demands become psychologically, emotionally and physically overwhelming. The diagnosis today that most closely resembles a breakdown is major depression, or in lay terms, a mental health crisis.

Just like the Phoenix, in the mighty grips of depression I was reduced to a pile of ashes. I became a completely different person—a virtual non-entity. I did not want to work. I could not sleep. I could not concentrate. Those areas in which I usually excelled became exercises in futility. I completely shut down, further withdrew from all feeling and emotion, and literally ceased to carry out all but the most crucial tasks in order to keep a roof over my head and sustain my basic needs.

While I desperately wanted to return to my "old" self and shake off this heavy burden, the depression was too far gone and I was too lethargic to do anything about it. Merely getting out of bed each morning took every ounce of strength that I could muster, and I forced myself to get dressed, show up for work and maintain a pleasant disposition to the degree possible—and that did not always go well given my uncontrollable bouts of irritability and agitation.

I began to isolate myself from the people and activities that I once enjoyed. In my state of social isolation, I would go out for long walks after work, not connecting with anyone or anything around me. I just wanted to be left alone, and I walked and walked and walked with no clear thoughts or destination in mind. There was no consoling me, and it was during this time that I became consumed by a preoccupation with death, because it seemed like the only way out of my dark oppression. I had not considered *how* I wanted to die, I just knew that I was hanging onto life by a thin and fragile thread and desperately wanted the intense psychological pain to end.

After months of this debilitating distress, one evening my world came crashing down. I went out and bought a bottle of sleeping pills and alcohol before going to a group therapy session for eating disorders. (Yes, I developed a temporary eating disorder, but that is another story for another book.) On this particular evening, I did not feel like going through the motions of sitting through a session. So I called our group therapist to indicate that I would not be attending. She sensed my distress and talked me into participating in the meeting despite my feelings, because I needed to be in community with the group. I cannot explain why I did not ignore her and immediately take the pills, but something forced me to put my demise on hold until after our session. I now know that it was my final cry for help.

Upon arrival at our group session, I was deeply agitated, unfocused and disconnected from others and myself. I was completely numb and still trying to hang onto that mask of perfection, but in the midst of my anguish it was being stripped away by the minute. Not being able to contain my restless spirit any longer, I announced that I was so tired of living this way, and wanted out—NOW! I felt ashamed for even having suicidal thoughts, but I needed to tell someone. Then I crumbled in a sobbing inconsolable heap right there on the floor.

Having reached the lowest and most painful point in my life, I was desperate to escape any way that I could.

Although I had never actually attempted suicide, that night I came daringly close and the pronouncement landed me a month-long stay in a psychiatric hospital.

I distinctly remember our group therapist calling my primary therapist requesting that she meet us at the hospital right away, then driving me there to check in sometime around midnight. Despite my incessant crying and protests, they had no other options. Both therapists were well aware of my potential and intentions to end my life, so admitting me into the hospital was the best course of action given the dire state that I was in.

Upon admittance, I was assigned a private room with no mirrors or anything else that I might use to harm myself. The staff checked on me regularly throughout the night. I was an absolute wreck, as the dark angel of death hovered over me. Feeling so hopeless and helpless, the tears continued to fall, and that is when the dam burst. I cried non-stop for hours. I cried for every feeling and every emotion that I had ever swallowed and refused to confront. I cried some more for sadness, anger, frustration, disappointment, confusion, fear, anxiety and bitterness. I was scared, emotionally scarred, hollow, lost and disengaged from myself, and the world around me. That first night, lying there in my hospital bed—all alone—was the lowliest and loneliest night of my life.

During the first several days of my stay, I was psychologically fragile and emotionally vulnerable. I refused to get out of bed, eat, leave my room, participate in group sessions and creative activities or accept visitors — even members of my own family. I even tried once, unsuccessfully, to escape. During these early days, the staff

43

did not force me to come out of my self-imposed prison to interact with others, but allowed me the time and space to just *be*.

In addition to psychotherapy, one of the unique interventions used in my hospital treatment was art therapy, a creative process and effective tool in enhancing mental and emotional well-being. A pottery class was the expressive medium that helped induce a sense of calmness as I explored various aspects of my personality to sharpen self-awareness, gain insight, increase self-esteem, develop interpersonal skills, manage my behavior and overcome psychological and emotional distress.

Through developing artistic self-expression, I shaped, formed, glazed and fired three small ceramic bears that represented my deep evolutionary process as I began to confront and express some of my feelings and emotions. I still have those bears today as a constant reminder of where God has brought me from in terms of my own evolution.

Breakthrough – A Spiritual Renaissance

A BREAKTHROUGH IS the sudden knowledge or insight that emerges after struggling for a period to understand something. I can best illustrate this concept by once again returning to the mythical Phoenix, the immortal bird that symbolizes rebirth. After death, the Phoenix is reduced to ashes, but it is reborn anew to live another 500 to 1,000 years. Rising from my ashes represented new life after the devastation that affected me internally—miracles, momentum and manifestation.

No other literary piece captures the essence of my breakdown and subsequent breakthrough like that of *Renascence*, a poem written in 1912 by 20-year-old Edna St. Vincent Millay (1892–1950). The poem, originally entitled *Renaissance* (meaning new birth), exposes the poet's vulnerability and describes her dramatic personal spiritual awakening from death to resurrection. It encapsulates one of the deepest mysteries of the universe —our inner conflicting forces of the will to live and the will to die.

In 1923, Millay became the first woman to win the Pulitzer Prize for poetry. Ironically, the author herself suffered a psychological breakdown and temporarily stopped writing, but she eventually continued writing through the encouragement and support of her husband.

After hospitalization, and as I continued working my way through the healing process, I carried a copy of this poem in my wallet, posted a copy on my refrigerator, and kept a copy on my nightstand. I read it over and over and over again, and wept each time. In an odd kind of way, I felt that Edna St. Vincent Millay was a kindred spirit who lived and died years before I was born. Her words gave me daily comfort and strength knowing that she had a very similar experience and was able to articulate it in such a powerful and moving way. Contemplating life from a mountaintop, she carries us through her personal suffering and spiritual awakening.

The last verse of the lengthy piece speaks volumes and continues to resonate with me today in untold ways as I reflect on my own breakdown and subsequent transformation.

"The soul can split the sky in two,
and let the face of God shine through...
And he whose soul is flat
— the sky will cave in on him by and by."

~ Edna St. Vincent Millay

The world we live in reinforces getting into our head and staying there, so it takes concentrated effort to connect with the innermost parts of ourselves. Yet, to become grounded we must get out of our heads and into our hearts. I encourage you to read and reread this poem in its entirety and then sit with it to gain a deeper sense of its meaning and relationship to humanity. In doing so, I hope you will find it as captivating and empowering as I have.

Knocked Down, but Not Out

EVERYONE FEELS SAD or blue at times, but these feelings usually pass within a few days. Major depression lingers indefinitely and is a real and serious illness that interferes with and reduces an individual's quality of life. According to a 2012 National Institute of Mental Health study, an estimated 16 million American adults (age 18 and older) had at least one major depressive episode in the previous year, representing 6.9 percent of all U.S. adults.

It is also interesting to note that while depression affects both men and women, it is more commonly diagnosed in women. The reasons are not entirely clear, because there are a number of factors—including biological, psychological, cultural and social—that must be considered. The reality remains, however, that as women, we must develop an awareness of what we might possibly face.

Symptoms of Depression

DEPRESSION VARIES FROM person to person and manifests in different ways. It can occur once in your lifetime, or it can be a chronic illness accompanied by feelings of emptiness and despair that have taken over your life and prevent you from enjoying a quality existence. The symptoms of depression include, but are not limited to: anxiety; extreme mood swings; lethargy; social and emotional isolation; insomnia; appetite changes; persistent aches and pains; and suicidal thoughts, threats or attempts.

If you can identify with several of these signs and symptoms, you might be suffering from depression. While I did not experience all of the above symptoms during my early episodes of depression, I did strongly identify with most of them.

Causes of Depression

WHILE THE EXACT cause of depression is unknown, there are many contributing factors that are now known: *Genetics* (family history), *chemical* (unbalanced brain neurotransmitters), *hormonal* (imbalances such as menopause, thyroid problems and viruses), and *social* factors (traumatic events, death, relationship and financial problems, and social pressures) all intersect to drive depression.

A chemical imbalance is the primary cause of my depression, which can be exacerbated by hormonal and social factors. Each person is different and it is often a combination of factors that contribute to depression. Therefore, it is important to recognize the symptoms and causes and seek professional treatment.

Treatment Options and Sources

DEPRESSION IS A highly treatable mental illness. However, dealing with depression is made more difficult because of social stigma and myths associated with the condition. The more you understand the causes, nature and symptoms of depression, the better able you are to treat it. Also, the earlier you seek treatment, the more effective and greater the likelihood that recurrences can be prevented or managed.

If you think you may be experiencing a mental health crisis, do not allow fear, guilt or shame to prevent you from getting the help that you need. There are numerous tools, resources and treatment options available including medication, psychotherapy, electroconvulsive therapy, hormone replacement therapy and alternative treatments. I recognize and have accepted that my *depression cannot be overcome, but it can be managed.* Proof: my personal treatment options have been largely confined to medication, psychotherapy, and alternative treatments such as aromatherapy, massage, prayer and meditation, nutrition and exercise. I feel so fortunate; not since the hospitalization in my mid-20s, have I experienced another episode of depression that was as intense or lasted for so long.

While there are many treatment options available, the key is to find a combination that works for you. To accomplish that, a thorough evaluation is required by a licensed professional who can prescribe a treatment plan that is aligned with your individual circumstances and needs.

There are also many good sources that provide information, tools and resources about depression: family physicians, hospitals, clinics, mental health practitioners, employee assistance programs, community centers, religious organizations and peer support groups. This list is in no way exhaustive, but it does offer a starting point in terms of seeking mental health assistance.

If you are suffering from depression and feel reluctant to contact a professional resource, I encourage you to reach out to someone that you trust to help guide you in the right direction to get the information, assistance and support that you need.

A Divine Appointment and Full-Circle Moment

MY STORY DID not end after being released from the hospital 25 years ago. In fact, this year—a quarter of a century later—it came full circle. In January, I was invited

49

to join the organization, Women on Fire (WOF) by a wonderful fellow member whom I have never physically met but with whom I have spiritually connected. Upon joining the organization, I discovered that they were hosting their annual retreat in Naples, Florida in late February/early March of this year. Before attending such events, I usually conduct some preliminary research and get to know the organization better. However, I felt a strange, inexplicable and pressing need to attend this retreat; so I discussed it with my husband, completed my registration and made travel arrangements. I would soon learn that I had a Divine appointment to be in attendance at this retreat.

I generally do not concern myself with what people think or say about me. However, when you get caught in a downward spiral that takes you to the place of wanting to end your life, go out and buy the pills, and then have to be hospitalized to prevent you from following through on your plan, it generates some very uneasy feelings and causes a significant amount of stress and anxiety. I arrived in Naples for the WOF Retreat feeling this stress and anxiety and my mind was screaming for clarity about whether or not to share my story in this book. That is when I started talking to God.

As I lay in bed the night before the retreat, I thought to myself that there are times when I wonder if God really hears me when I talk to Him, so I told Him so. I said, "God, sometimes, I do not think you hear me when I talk to you. You know I am supposed to co-author *Miracles, Momentum and Manifestation*, but I am struggling with whether or not to go public with my bottom-fell-out-story in this book. In fact, I am really, really, REALLY scared and

50

wondering, *What will people think? What will they say? How will this impact my professional reputation and effectiveness?* If YOU want me to share this particular story at this point in my life, then YOU will have to make it clear. Actually, You will have to make it CRYSTAL clear, so that I can move forward with this project without any doubt, knowing that You have ordained it to be so." After talking to God, I turned out the light, rolled over and went to sleep. I had no earthly idea that the very next morning He would answer – and that His answer would be not just clear, but CRYSTAL clear.

After a good night's sleep, I arose the next morning with no preconceived ideas or expectations about the retreat. I showered, dressed and headed downstairs to register and collect my name badge and retreat materials. Instead of eating a full breakfast, I grabbed a cup of coffee and proceeded to our meeting room to find a comfortable seat to enjoy my coffee and a meal replacement bar without drawing any unnecessary attention to myself. Since this was my first WOF retreat and my first time meeting this particular group of women, I wanted to keep a low profile and go with the flow. But God had a completely different plan.

When I sat down in our meeting room I did not immediately review the materials in my retreat bag. So mid-morning, just before we were about to break out into small group circles, I had this overwhelming urge to take a look at the participant list. I pulled out the list, quickly scanned it, and my hometown suddenly caught my attention.

I followed the line over to the participant's name and knowing no one else in the area by this name, it dawned on me that she *had* to be the same person who had driven me to the hospital on that dreadful night 25 years ago after I announced my suicide intentions during the support group that she was leading.

Upon seeing this participant's name, my mind immediately took me back to that night of desperation as if it had happened only yesterday, and I began to tremble all over and lose my composure. With wobbly knees, a rapid heart beat, dry mouth and sweaty palms, I got out of my seat, walked up to the WOF Founder, who was standing at the edge of the stage, and asked her if she would point out this individual to me, because I had just spotted her name on the participant list. The Founder's response was, *"She's standing right behind you."* I turned around, and there stood the participant—the same woman that I remembered from so many years ago.

At that moment, you could have knocked me over with a feather. Here I am, 25 years after the most traumatic experience of my life, standing face-to-face with the woman who played a significant role in saving me from ending my life. Mere words can never convey the astonishment that overcame me as I stood before and reconnected with the woman who played such a pivotal role in my history.

I am usually very poised in public settings, but with so many thoughts running through my mind I was now feeling a bit of hysteria. My heart was racing and I could feel myself about to become unglued. For the first time ever, I found myself publicly sharing the one story that I had protected for so long and been so fearful of discussing. Not only did I share my story, I shared it with a room full of women whom I was meeting for the very first time... and I did it in the midst of an unexpected and full-blown ugly cry accompanied by running mascara, smeared make-up, a snotty nose and a crinkled face.

Surprisingly, I did not focus on how I looked, because a Power greater than myself had taken over. I cannot recall everything that I conveyed, but do know that a good amount of my buried story was resurrected right then and there. And I have been told many times that it inspired virtually every woman in that room!

I asked God to make things CRYSTAL clear, and He answered. It was not in the way that I had anticipated, but He answered... leaving me with no doubt that mustering courage to share such a difficult personal story was what He intended for me to do to inspire souls who have given out and given up, as well as those who are lost and desperately trying to find their way.

Each Day is an Opportunity to Begin Anew

THE EGO IS a key part of being human, but it is just one aspect of our core being. If we are not careful, the ego will overtake and convince us that it reins supreme as our primary source of identity, sustenance, protection and survival. When we allow the ego to attach itself to our thoughts, attitudes and behaviors, it causes us to deny the very essence of who we are. Overcoming ego's hold on us requires a shift in perception. It requires us to let go of our self-centeredness and embrace a higher calling that promotes the greater good of humanity.

I continue to be a work in progress, but the superficial mask that I had so meticulously erected early in life has slowly cracked and diminished over the years in my quest to experience the fullness of life. Through it all, I have gained momentum by becoming more self-aware and more authentic and I give thanks daily for the strength, endurance and wisdom that have miraculously manifested and continue to manifest through my life's unpredictable twists and turns.

Each day presents an opportunity for me to renew the vow to myself to transform fear into courage. I still have to make a concerted effort to let some things go and often find myself asking, *"What is holding me back? What do I need to let go of? What am I finished with and what is finished with me? Why am I afraid to let go? What will happen if I let go?"* But by and by, my safety net appears – and usually at the most unexpected time and in the most unexpected way—to enlarge my faith and trust in my Creator, and nurture a spirit of gratitude.

Life's path is not always narrow and neat, but sometimes wide and messy. While a state of brokenness draws pain, from it emerges mighty things. In relating this story, I am remembering how far I have come, not just how far I have to go. While I am not where I want to be, I am certainly not where I used to be. Life has presented me with some challenging and traumatic experiences that seemed as though they would never end, but what I know for sure is that the human spirit is resilient; and if we are open to receive the lessons, our souls will transform our suffering into joy.

As I reflect on the miracles in my life, I am acutely aware that we reach a point in life when it becomes not just clear, but *crystal* clear that we have traveled too far to turn around. Regardless of what beckons us from our past, we can no longer think, do, say or be any aspect of our former self, because we have now outgrown that stage. When we are called to this higher place, there is simply no denying it. Our only option is to gather up our courage and walk confidently through the door that has been so generously and unexpectedly opened right before us to embrace our next phase of life.

Oftentimes when we ask for a miracle, we doubt that it will manifest. I requested quite a few miracles when my life was a wreck, and I always received them even though I did not understand the fullness of them at the time. Today, I can unequivocally tell you that miracles do happen. Every one of our life experiences—no matter how painful—has a purpose. We may not understand that purpose during the dark times, but everything unfolds exactly the way and at the precise moment it is supposed to. If I ever doubted whether or not God hears and answers my prayers, He has proven to me in no small way that He loves me and has my back as I continue to travel this journey called life; and I am eternally grateful.

Perhaps you are walking around as a hollow shell stuck in an emotional valley. Or maybe you are holding on to a buried story that you have never shared with another living soul, and it is robbing you of peace. If you need a miracle manifested in your life, *ask* (that's how you gain

55

momentum), and trust and believe that the Universe hears you and will deliver. Then release the fear and allow it to dissolve into thanksgiving. Just like the Phoenix, rise up from your ashes knowing that whatever you endured happened for a reason and you survived it to enhance your growth, make you stronger and be a beacon of light and an inspiration to others. Stay strong and be encouraged, because regardless what you have been through or what you are going through, your best days are yet to come... and *that* in itself is a miracle!

About the Author

DR. MARY CANTY MERRILL has spent more than 25 years motivating and inspiring audiences across the country to step out of their comfort zone and into their personal power. In addition to entrepreneur and psychologist, she is blessed to serve humanity in a variety of roles. As an educator, facilitator, speaker, author, and life strategist, she is known for her thought-provoking messages, high-energy delivery, and dynamic work in unleashing human potential.

She partners with numerous Fortune 500 companies, government and non-profit agencies, educational institutions, individuals, groups and communities to inspire new levels of confidence, productivity, performance and success. To stimulate fresh insights and transformative life experiences, Mary is intentional about continuous self-improvement and is a regularly featured guest on radio talk shows. She is also the co-author of an anthology, *The Daughters and Spirit of Harriet* and is currently working on her third soon-to-be-released book, *Realm of Revelation*.

Follow Dr. Merrill at:

www.merrillca.com
www.mcantymerrill.wordpress.com
https://twitter.com/mcantymerrill
https://www.facebook.com/MerrillConsultingAssociates
http://www.amazon.com/dp/1491870850

Chapter 4

THE MIRACLE OF MAN-I-FESTING THE ULTIMATE LOVE RELATIONSHIP!

Mamiko Odegard, Ph.D.

*Keep love in your heart.
The consciousness of loving and
being loved brings warmth and
richness to life that nothing else can
bring.*

~Oscar Wilde

IT COULD BE said by some that to manifest a beautiful and lasting relationship would be something akin to a miracle. That need not be your reality. Do you dream of having a loving relationship with the perfect partner in which you feel cherished, are treated tenderly, passionately, and regarded as the most important person in the world? It is possible to shift from "wishing and hoping" to using a tried and true blueprint to "MAN-ifest" the kind of love, respect, and devotion you deeply crave. If you're ready to go for the gold, then read on, and let's build some momentum in your quest for an ultimate LOVE relationship.

My husband, Greg, and I have been blessed with a loving and magical marriage for over 40 years. When we met, it was almost love at first sight. Greg's loving ways confirm to me each day of how cherished I am by him. However, for many years I was self-consciousness about my Japanese appearance and the secrets that I kept hidden... I always wondered if I would find my true love and find the love I had to give reciprocated.

Falling in love with Greg was indeed a miracle and blessing from God. When I immigrated to the Unites States from Japan, from the beginning I was taunted and made fun of my appearance and ethnicity. I quickly learned to be ashamed and self-conscious of my cultural background and Asian looks. Furthermore, because I didn't understand the language and was unable to read or write English, I felt ashamed that I was behind academically, struggling with both reading and math.

My father was in the military and he was relocated several times during the early years. Each time he was transferred to a different city, I was moved up a grade. The academic rigors finally caught up with me in the fourth grade when I failed it and had to repeat. I kept this a secret until my adulthood. As I became older, I quickly became aware of the negative stereotypes about Asians being nerdy, shy, emotionally repressed, and uncommunicative. Almost from the beginning of my arrival here, I began to distance myself more from my Japanese heritage. I became the "banana;" yellow on the outside and white on the inside. Yes, I thought, felt, and acted as a WASP, as I desperately sought to fit in with my white, socially acceptable and popular friends.

My first home in the States was a one-bedroom house that my parents rented. I slept on the sofa or in my parent's bed. As I became older, I added even more layers of shame. During that memorable fourth grade, we lived right next door to the elementary school that I attended. We occupied a one-bedroom apartment and had to use a common bathroom that was down the hall. I was embarrassed to invite my classmates to my home, because I still slept on the sofa or in my parent's bed. As I look back on it now, I find it interesting that my best friends were ones who were bussed and lived in beautiful, classy, wealthy homes and neighborhoods.

When I was 10, our family was finally able to buy our first two-bedroom home in a "respectable" neighborhood in Boise, Idaho. I felt so ecstatic to finally have my own room and quickly made friends with the two girls living close by. Unfortunately, having this coveted separate bedroom became a liability for me, as my father began to sexually molest me and use me as his confidant and surrogate wife. Again, another secret that I had to endure, because my parents were so volatile, and no social support systems existed at that time.

My father had served in every branch of the service except the Navy. Whenever, my father switched his military allegiance, he lost rank. Consequently, when I was in junior high and high school, he was still a staff sergeant. In contrast, my middle school and older friends were from prosperous families whose fathers were professionals and successful entrepreneurs and mothers were homemakers. I was readily accepted and befriended by my peers due to my friendly, funny, loyal nature with great social and communication skills. Although I didn't have problems attracting dates, I would cringe every time I would meet the parents, especially when they would ask me what my father did. I could easily detect their disdain toward our family; that I was not good enough for their son. Adding to the humiliation was the fact that my mother worked as a waitress for several years before she began managing a card and gift store.

It is noteworthy, that during those years when I felt inadequate socio-economically, "like damaged goods" due to the repeated sexual abuse, my Asian looks, and my failing the fourth grade, I NEVER disliked myself. Instead I liked and loved the person that I was and was grateful for my attractive personality and appearance. I always felt that I deserved the very best that life had to offer.

I was destined to find a path for myself to totally accept who I was, my culture, my background, and my family. I was also destined to find ways to love and forgive my father for his actions. Despite his verbal, physical, and sexual abuse, I knew that he truly loved me and was very proud of me. As I grew older, I realized the many feelings of inadequacy that he held.

There is no mere coincidence that I had a loving heart and was genuinely caring of others that led me to the fields of counseling and coaching. I have spent my whole life fine tuning self-esteem, self-love, and developing deep, lasting, profound relationships with others. Thus, when Greg and I met, I had already been evolving to "my best self," knowing and acting on the belief that I could achieve what I set as my heart's goal and that I was worthy and deserved a man who could treat me with respect, tenderness, and would love me forever. In fact, to show you my sense of humor (I didn't know about positive affirmations or treasure-mind mapping back then), I had a colorful postcard over my bed in my college apartment that said, "College, a warm place between high school and marriage!"

Joking aside, Greg accepted me fully as I was. This was because as our trust and love grew, we became best friends, sharing our inner most secrets. When I shared mine, Greg was unconditionally loving and even more appreciative of the person that I was. Yes, his total love and acceptance catapulted me to feel that I was safe in releasing my secrets and validated my worthiness. For that, I am deeply grateful to Greg.

The most important message here is to develop your best self, to know and feel that you are extraordinary to attract your true loving partner... and when you find him or her, to be proactive in the small daily gestures of love to show how much your partner means to you. Love can easily fade through the years. Our marriage is a testament that a relationship can retain love, passion, appreciation, freshness, and respect far beyond courting and the early years of marriage.

Revealing my proven secrets to having the "ultimate" love, the following blueprint is a formula for attracting and keeping love vibrant and growing over time.

Create the Best Version of Yourself; be EXTRA-ordinary.

ALL CHANGE BEGINS with awareness... rest assured, you hold the power to attract and keep a vibrant, cherished love forever. It is about creating the best version of yourself in which you know that you are indeed extraordinary. Remember, Greg and I were attracted to each other, primarily because of the positive energies of our feelings—and actions to confirm and elevate our self worth, liking, and loving ourselves and the capacity for loving others.

Repeatedly, over the course of over 40 years of counseling and coaching individuals, a truth has been revealed: *Unless you accept and love yourself, and hold yourself as being valuable with high esteem, unconsciously you undermine yourself.* Yes, that's right, you prevent yourself from achieving your highest career and life goals and find yourself attracting and being attracted to persons who continually let you down. In other words, **you cannot outperform your self-esteem**. Furthermore, no one else can elevate your worth and lovability. If you don't feel valuable, attractive, and important to your partner, no amount of physical affection, words of love, or even sex can fill that emptiness of disbelief of your own feelings of preciousness and being prioritized and loved by another.

You might have also noticed that when you don't fully love yourself, you tend to hear a critical, self-sabotaging, harsh voice that routinely puts you down. Automatically, the voice inside your head reacts to those around you with the same deprecating and judgmental tone. This is why it's so essential to learn to be gentle, nurturing, and supportive of yourself first.

When you are generous with yourself, you can also give others the benefit of doubt and be able to views their intentions and actions in loving ways. For instance, a husband might devote much of his energies to his work. You are left with a man who's too tired at night to give you the attention, conversation, physical affection, and compliments you crave.

It's common to think that he doesn't love you, because he has nothing left in the tank for you. However, you might be surprised at his reaction when you compliment, hug, and kiss him for working so hard for you and the family. Instantly he gets it that you understand and appreciate that he shows love to you by working so hard.

One way to think about in changing the critical inner voice to one of gentle acceptance is to view yourself "re-parenting" the child within by giving yourself the love, compassion, and encouragement you may have missed out on as a child. You can make a conscious choice now to be a tender adult rather than believing that you must adhere to tough standards of performance in which you must be near perfect to gain praise, acceptance and love. As you begin to talk and think differently in more loving ways – with respect and cherishing – you will find you begin to manifest these same behaviors from those around you... and you are on your way to being your best self.

It's Okay to be Selfish!

MANY OF YOU have been taught that you should put other's needs, wants, and well-being in front of you. The problem remains however, when you neglect your own needs and wants; you frequently feel unimportant, tired, discouraged, sad, and victimized. You are often so busy taking care of others; you even lose sight of and are not in touch with your own feelings and needs. Feeling at times like a victim, you allow others and events to control your life, further leading to emotions of hopelessness, anxiety, irritability, resentment, and powerlessness.

There's a big difference between being egocentric and self-absorbed to acting on your behalf and being "self-full." Taking care of yourself is a major facet of loving and prioritizing yourself enough to make sure your own needs are being met. Only when you do so, can you truly love yourself and others. Otherwise, you do things for others, and have nothing left in the tank to nurture and take care of your own needs. Obviously, thinking that your lover, husband, family, friend, or co-worker will be able to accurately guess at your needs and take steps to fulfill them are not reality based. Only you have the true access to fulfill your own happiness and well-being.

This is why it is absolutely okay and encouraged that you meet your own needs and wants through self-care. In doing so, you actually provide a gift of love to those all around you, because you are happier, lighter, warmer, more fun, and pleasant to be around. After all, emotions are highly contagious—Wouldn't you want to share love and joy rather than complaining and being devoid of energy, life, and fulfillment?

To be truly successful in nurturing, loving, and prioritizing yourself, you must identify the beliefs that undermine your efforts for treating yourself gently and allowing yourself to put your needs before others. These beliefs are often formed early in our families; often certain rules or beliefs are unspoken but certainly demonstrated. For instance, was your mother the one who continually sacrificed herself and put everyone else's needs ahead of her own? No matter your past, you can start now with adopting and choosing to embrace new more functional beliefs. The power is in your hands to manifest true love and happiness!

Learn The Art of Mindful Loving

MINDFULLNESS IS DEFINED as moment-to-moment awareness—without judgment. As discussed earlier, are you accepting or critical of yourself and others? If so, this is an important life lesson to learn and develop.

Imagine for every situation, your mind's eye carries a powerful high-speed camera, capable of taking multiple photos within a millisecond. The goal is to be calm enough for you to take a moment to view different ways of perceiving or interpreting a particular situation. For instance, your significant other has not called or texted you today. One reaction might be "I can't believe he hasn't called or texted. He's not thinking of me... I'm not important enough to him."

Another way of thinking about this same situation might be: "Hmmm, Larry hasn't called or texted today. I wonder if he's bogged down with work." Obviously, you are going to have totally different emotions of irritation, disappointment, hurt, and sadness with the former personalized thinking. In contrast, the second way of perceiving the same situation, results in more positive feelings of care and concern toward the other person.

The art of mindful loving is a skill that is developed like a muscle. The more you expand the way you view situations in a nonjudgmental way, the more enlightened you become and more capable of accepting with a greater capacity for love and warmth. Being critical and judgmental are replaced by neutrality and thoughts that give you and others the "benefit of doubt," which in turn allows the best intentions to spring forth.

Remember moment-to-moment means being in the present moment and looking at situations with clear, new eyes. This means that if you are ever critical or judgmental of yourself and others—immediately STOP! That's right, learn to stop in your tracks and view the situations through different lenses of that magical camera, your brain, and strive for neutrality. You don't have to be positive or the cheerleader. Instead, the goal is to be more accepting and neutral in the ways you view circumstances. In turn, your emotions reward you with joy, comfort, acceptance, patience, and greater displays of love in feeling and actions.

The skill of mindful loving is exactly that – a skill. At first you may find yourself going back to your past reactions of recrimination and pain. Initially, you may find these new ways of reframing and thinking more difficult, even with much conscious effort. However, with greater awareness and desire, you catch yourself and make the correction more quickly with time. The more you can remind yourself to look at situations in a neutral way or with more favorable connotations, the greater will be your ability to show love to yourself and others.

Please do not be harsh on yourself while you learn these skills; they ripen and develop with time and use so that the behavior begins to become more natural and automatic for you. Start loving yourself first and let that love flow towards your loved ones.

Show Love Multiple Times in Many Ways

YOU CAN CREATE opportunities each day to show your love in physical, emotional, verbal, and spiritual ways. You may often believe that you can only show love at certain times, such as hugging and kissing each other when you leave for work or come home. In actuality, you can demonstrate love in diverse ways throughout the day to communicate: "You are my one and only; I love and cherish you; I'm so happy to be with you; no one makes me laugh like you do!"

These sentiments are easily expressed verbally. However, the combination of verbal and physical make an even greater impact on those whose hearts you want to touch. The next time you kiss and hug, try mentioning your favorite phrases of appreciation, recognition, love, and gratitude and see what responses from your beloved you receive in turn.

Your skin is the largest organ in your body. **Make sure to touch each other daily** by rubbing the back, massaging the neck and shoulders, caressing each other or holding hands while watching television, and offering multiple hugs and kisses throughout the day. Touch is not necessarily about sex. There are two different types of touch:

The first one is the one that you can associate from your earliest memories of being held or touched that automatically cause you to relax while your body rewards you by slowing down. You can see this in babies as well as when you are cuddling or having the rhythmic, slow stroking of your head, back, or feet. This type of touch is intended to help you to soothe and relax each other physically and emotionally.

The second type of touch invigorates, stimulates, and ignites you physically, sexually, emotionally, and mentally. Think of the last time you kissed when you felt aroused and alive physically. Even when you remember the closeness of your bodies, feeling the breath, and heartbeat of the other, your mind can quickly recreate the moment and the excitement. What's even more important is that your love extends through space in time... your loved one can also actually feel that closeness and passion too as he recalls your time together.

Love can be demonstrated through other physical acts that make life easier and more pleasant for another, such as taking out the garbage without reminders or requests, bringing your special one a beverage of his or her choice as you return from the kitchen, cleaning the home, yard, or car, and filling up the car with gas. These acts of love speak volumes of the consideration, thoughtfulness, and kindness you have for another. Remember "love is a verb" helps you to show love and kindness through action, and sends a strong message of your tenderness and caring.

The quality of the time you spend together is another way of showing love. When you are cuddling next to each other, enjoying activities together, laughing and being playful, or engaged in deep intimate conversation, you are setting the stage to enhance the special moments you do share. You may not remember exactly what you or your beloved said or did at times, but you definitely remember how you felt in each other's company.

When my husband was working out of state and commuting back home every Friday evening, our time together was too precious to squander it arguing or being disgruntled with the other. We learned to quickly put aside our differences or to resolve them to avoid spoiling the weekend together. That's why our goal was to make every weekend a "honeymoon weekend," filled with fun and rejuvenating activities together as a couple as well as with our daughter.

Sometimes, the quality of time, is just with yourself, enjoying private moments to sleep, refresh, and to pursue your own activities that might be different that your beloved's. After all, you can have more fun and more to talk about with your loved ones when you have your own interests and activities.

Still another way to show love is to make or purchase gifts. We tend to think of gift giving during occasions such as Valentine's Day, Easter, Mother's Day, Father's Day, birthdays, anniversaries, and holidays. However, gifts have the most impact when given spontaneously from the heart for no special occasion when they convey, "I love you." Gifts might be an attractive shirt you know your partner would love, a live plant, or a favorite pastry or snack that pleasantly surprises the lucky recipient. A heartfelt gift might also include a poem or love letter, or even a text message that is spicy and romantic.

A guaranteed way to show love and deepen any relationship is to share your true thoughts and feelings with your beloved. Allowing yourself to be open and wanting your partner to know the real you, creates the ultimate trust and love for both yourself and your partner. The ability to share creates interdependence and intimacy—allowing the other to "see into you"—as well as knowing and feeling that your mate understands and supports you, and has your back to protect and stand up for you. The level of disclosure and the exchange of communication ensure that you can be yourself. When you both practice inter-dependence, either of you can ask for help and know you can rely on each other for assistance in good times and bad.

When Greg and I sent out our wedding invitations, the photo that we used was that of a tree growing toward the sky, intertwining it's branches, as if growing into one. That symbolism is still so relevant today, because over time, we have actually grown together, combining our interests, talents, skills, and personality while we maintained our own individual sense of uniqueness—becoming even stronger when united. You can too!

Obviously the empathy that you demonstrate toward one another and the level and quality of your communication between you also creates closer bonds between you. They also contribute to your quality of time together. When you are cuddling, laughing, or sharing your inner most thoughts and feelings while being understood by each other, these loving connections all add up to how well your time is spent as a couple.

Next time you go for a "date" with your lover, pretend that this is the first time you are meeting. Reminisce and talk about how you met, what you talked about, what intrigued you about the other... and if you're feeling frisky, flirt with your partner, being captivating, and finding out more about the other—even after all the years. Go for a game of smiles and laughter and see how well your evening turns out!

Learn The Signs Your Beloved Gives You

YOUR PARTNER UNCONSCIOUSLY provides clues for you as to whether he or she is approaching you or distancing from you. It's important to recognize when and how you approach and avoid your partner. You might begin to think of these signals as traffic lights of green, yellow, and red that denote whether to precede full speed ahead, to utilize caution, or to stop what you are doing.

When you are friendly—greeting your partner with a warm embrace, kiss, and messages of "I'm so happy to see you,"—you will notice a definite "green" light. Your beloved perks up, reciprocates in his or her own form of affection, and matches your energy of love and excitement to be with you. Time together is magical and seems to slip away too soon.

When you are sensing "yellow" light your partner provides signals that he or she is starting to back away or becoming disengaged from you. Some signs include not listening, looking away, a general sense of being disinterested, and becoming overly or abruptly quiet. For instance, you excitedly talk about different places you'd like to travel that are on your bucket list. You may not notice, that all the sudden, your partner becomes quiet, less animated, and less engaged with you. Your loved one may be thinking there is no way to provide those types of vacations for you, and begins to feel inadequate or that he or she has failed you.

If you notice this type of withdrawal or yellow light, you can then use it as an opportunity to turn your conversation and engagement to green. You might make a comment such as, "I noticed as I was talking about vacations, you became quiet." This provides an opening for your partner to say how he or she feels and the reason for pulling back from you. Women often notice this whenever they bring up the topic of taking a relationship to the next level of commitment.

A "red light" is when you can visibly see that your partner is backing away or becoming disengaged. He or she might become quickly agitated, short-tempered, yell, become angry, defensive, and accusatory, slam a door, name call, or leave. Red lights may erupt quickly, but you can have an agreement that if there is ever any situation that causes distress to that level, each of you will be honest and open with the other.

Sometimes in red light situations one or both parties may find it helpful to have a "time out" to regain calm to better understand and express thoughts and feelings. Bear in mind: *remaining calm is a pathway to mindful loving, to be able to perceive or think in such a way that you experience the best outcome.* When your emotions are highly charged, your thinking only parallels those feelings. In other words, if you are too angry and believe that it's your partner's fault, your thoughts will spontaneously and quickly tumble to those that justify your feelings. This is why it's so important to have some time out or even use time to write your thoughts and feelings. Once you cool down, then your mind more readily opens to others ways of thinking about yours and your partner's behaviors. "Giving the other the benefit of doubt," and allowing a more positive intention, is a supreme practice in mindful loving.

Dance The Masculine and Feminine Energy

THE HALLMARK OF a healthy relationship involves recognizing and embracing both male and female characteristics and behaviors. Typically desirable male characteristics involve being a leader, acting decisively, being analytical, problem and solution oriented, and taking care of his woman and children. Women's positive attributes frequently include nurturing, being a good communicator, gentle, patient, and giving. These feminine characteristics are not to be confused as being less desirable than their male counterparts. Instead, the dance of the masculine and female self is what both men and women desire. The "strong silent type" can only go so far. This stereotypical male is rigid and is unable to fully communicate his feelings or be able to demonstrate vulnerability.

If you go back to our discussion about showing love, the highest form of love and intimacy is to be yourself and share your innermost thoughts and feelings with another. Likewise, a woman needs to be assertive, to have a voice, and be empowered to make choices that help her reach her goals.

Too often more men and women are caught up in the typical masculine energy of being competitive, analytical, directive, controlling, and independent. Unfortunately, both the man and woman often maintain these roles and energies at home, creating friction with power struggles. As women have expanded in the workplace and assumed positions of power, they have enjoyed being empowered and making their own decisions. The man, on the other hand, might feel left out, not needed, intimidated, or disrespected as the woman in the relationship begins to make more of decisions for herself or her family... causing the boundaries of home and work to become blurred.

This can be even more of a slippery slope if the woman in the relationship is bringing home more money than her partner. Are you coming home and ordering your family around as if you are at work? Resentment surely will settle in, with your family tuning you out, avoiding you, or butting against your wishes.

I am not implying that women should be passive. In fact, it's the opposite. I want all of you to be in touch with your thoughts, feelings, needs, and wants. No one knows what you want. You don't want to allow the other to guess, because the results will be less than what you expect. When you are in the present awareness of all within you and around you, you have the freedom to express your desires, needs, and to ask for help. This is what interdependency is all about.

Again, you have a choice to assume the more feminine role regardless of whether you are a man or woman. Will you choose to be gentle, nurturing, cooperative, openly demonstrating love and doing the necessary dance of letting the other lead at times and going with the flow? Self-confidence, worthiness, esteem, and self love come into play, because when you feel extraordinary, you're less likely to feel threatened, irritated, and disappointed when your partner makes a decision.

You are also less likely to take his or her actions personally if an order is hastily barked out to you. Yes, the dance of the masculine and feminine energy is fluid and varies from situation to situation with your wants and interests balanced with your partner.

Have You Found the Perfect Partner and Attained the Ultimate Love?

DO YOU KNOW what makes a perfect partner, your soul mate? Does he or she possess the qualities and behaviors that have been discussed? If you want to determine how healthy and loving your relationship really is, go through the previous six key behaviors:

1. Develop your best self to be loving and accepting;
2. Become "self-full" and adopt new rules and beliefs that promote more beneficial feelings and outcomes;
3. Practice the art of mindfulness loving, striving to perceive your partner and situations in a more positive light and abstaining from judgment;
4. Show love in various ways throughout the day and night;
5. Become tuned to the signals of love or withdrawal that your loved one gives you; and
6. Do the dance of the male and female energy, going back and forth leading, following, and being in step with each other.

You are capable of great love... starting with yourself first! Enjoy creating your best self. You are extraordinary and you are on your way to true love.

After all, there's no feeling quite like being in love and being loved. Many blessings in MAN-ifesting love within yourself and your true partner.

About the Author

DR. MAMIKO ODEGARD, the love and relationship expert, and the founder of ACT on Love™, shares her unique, yet practical and tested secrets to love, teaching specific steps to achieve and retain the loving relationship(s) we all crave. The developer of a live workshop and CD series, entitled *Manthology 101: Manifesting Love,* Mamiko assists growing numbers of men and women seeking to find and keep healthy relationships and romantic love. Passionate about mentoring strong, successful, powerful woman to be connected to their leading man, she uses coaching programs and mixed singles groups to teach ways to break the ice and develop deep loving relations.

The world recognized Mamiko walks her talk as she and her husband, Greg, the love of her life, were chosen to be interviewed on Oprah Radio, The Dr. Laura Berman Show, as the Couple of the Week. She is also the best selling author of the widely acclaimed book, *Daily Affirmations for Love,* which details ways to show love 365 days of the year. The couple has a daughter, Mariesa, to complete their circle of love.

Join Dr. Mamiko as you ACT on Love:

http://www.ACTonLove.com
DrMamiko@ACTonLove.com
https://www.facebook.com/ACTOnLove
www.linkedin.com/pub/dr-mamiko-odegard/4/b65/140
http://www.amazon.com/Mamiko-Odegard-PhD/e/B004PHTA5A

Chapter 5

POSITIVELY DIVINE AND BEAUTIFULLY ABUNDANT... A RECIPE FOR LIFE

Valerie Sorrentino

ON OUR FINAL day in Italy, I pause as I sit back in first class—a reclining leather seat on the bullet train headed back to Rome. The day is breaking from the sleepy full night after our late "feast,"— typical Italian fare, with family, friends, wine, treats, and a language barrier we all laugh about.

My husband and I laugh at ourselves, too, for nearly missing the train after standing right in front of it for nearly half an hour while the sun rises.

I pause to slowly take in the earthy, beautiful surroundings of the abundant countryside. This trip has been good to me.

Is it a miracle?

Our journey has made my heart full and overflowing with joy. A stark contrast to the dark, dim, slow, painful night of the soul I was programmed to live out. My life has taken a new road, and look where it has led me today. Yes, it's a miracle to be sure!

In my last book, *{An} Unsinkable Soul*, I re-live the glimpse of a backward-moving spiral. I give a snapshot of a huge fall. I give a taste of the climb back up in *Miracles, Momentum and Manifestation* and share my journey to peace.

Looking out the window of the train, I see abundant crops filled with fruit, alive for sharing. I see the joy of cooking simply, eating plenty and caring deeply. My mind travels and I can see a picture of the momentum my life has taken on, the miracle that each day has become... from conscious manifestation. Each moment lean into manifesting happiness, living my truest truth every day.

To reveal myself truthfully feels like a miracle.

There was a time that I couldn't bear to admit my feelings of weakness to anyone, especially to myself. Weakness was never allowed. Perhaps illness was more acceptable. My body didn't know the difference. I now know the power and momentum of clarity, truth and deep relaxation. I know the miracle of healing.

I notice the landscape has become more littered than the tourist-rich towns. I overlook the colorful mounds of trash collecting on the roadsides and instead relish the ocean sounds, the comically manic traffic jams and active, celebratory lifestyle here in a simple land of southern Italy.

I choose my focus.

And remember how I arrived on this train . . .

I am thankful to pull my clumsy rolling bags over the uneven cobblestone streets before dawn, the sun barely visible as we race to find the train station down the street.

I'm mindful that the brisk, chilly early walk will help me digest the late night meal. I may never need to eat again, I laugh. In my perspective, each challenge offers a gift, each crossroad a grand opportunity. Each negative presents it's counterpart; a positive.

I find the gift in each moment.

The 4 o'clock hour of dawn, the additional three-hour train ride to catch a long flight home from Rome has its upside . . . yet to be seen. I'm sure it's there. It's called trusting in the unknown. This is a miracle, after all.

I stay in present time.

This morning's gift shows itself as I stand unknowingly in front of the train waiting for it to move along so that MY train may arrive. In the midst of the last five minutes before the train pulls away, in broken Italian, I learn THIS IS MY TRAIN!!! Ah, I find myself again panicky and racing to catch an open door before it departs. In fear of missing the train that will eventually get me home, I unearth a limiting belief that's riddled with stress. ***This inner panic doesn't feel like trust at all.***

How do I know that I have the limiting belief: *You have to race to catch a train and it may end in disaster?* Because this is the third time I've felt this way in a matter of ten days. That's what you call a pattern. This pattern is based on a belief. It keeps manifesting. It will show up again and again until I change my belief around it. Because I notice . . . well, in reality, I practice noticing . . . and in that awareness I know today is the day I will change this belief.

I practice awareness.

The belief that I may miss something... the belief that I am not at the right place at the right time... the belief that it has to be a close call, a struggle, and eventually, a relief. This is the gift, knowing I can clear this limiting pattern. In the moment, I recall:

Running for the train from Venice to Rome attracted gypsies and a chaotic scene with bags being slung here and there, losing track of our belongings. Running for the train from Rome to Salerno (while we had plenty of time but the same scary sensation of fear) encountered a better skill—watching out for gypsies. One showed up to lend a hand and we didn't let that happen again. Patterns offer opportunities to learn from and grow.

This morning, standing in front of the train, calmly waiting, early and on time—I'm oblivious that the very train I need to board is the one right in front of my face. In a flash of realization, we run eight cars forward to get to our seats, half laughing and half humbled by our beads of sweat.

I take a moment to notice—apparently this is a pattern. Swiftly, tapping into my body to feel what is lodged and rooted in fear, I clear the belief that we have to run in order to catch a train. With gratitude, I let it go.

I am deeply grateful.

Two examples before my story continues. **One:** Gaining momentum for manifesting miracles is an *action*. During my walk (a quick, brisk, early, dimly lit walk from hotel to train station) I had two choices:

1. Complain about the inconvenient _____ (fill in the blank), or,
2. Stay in deep, genuine gratitude for whatever is.

I chose the latter. I could feel the sliver of nervous energy that propelled me toward my track. I noticed the fear that arose with needing to catch a train and plane and a ride back to real life at home. My tremor was there for a purpose. However, I choose to stay in a grateful mindset, allowing the nerves to be my guide—unlike the need to only focus on the nerves, while being grateful for nothing and spinning out of center. Focusing on the negative brings a negative result. Awareness is the craft.

I listen to my body, mind and spirit.

In basic math principles, positive thinking creates positive momentum. Pluses. But one minus one does not equal two—it equals nothing. Zero. A negative.

Two: There will always be a positive and a negative that we have the choice on which to focus. It is always present. Slow down and choose wisely.

Gratitude is a great tool for moving energy forward. Forward-moving energy has great power and momentum. Negative thinking has great power as well. Negative momentum.

Look at what you are thinking and see how your thoughts and actions are interrelated. Negative momentum feels as if you are gaining nothing. No momentum, yet movement in the wrong direction. When the miracle arrives, you may miss it, because with negative distractions, the focus is placed elsewhere.

The miracle I see in myself is not that I caught the train. The miracle is not the actual sweet, seductive historical lands of Rome, Venice, Pisa, Florence, Portofino, Positano and Amalfi. The miracle is the true peace, joy and presence I have in the planning, preparing and participation of the long days, full nights, fast trains, feverish excursions and phenomenal tastings of the world. The miracle is that I am present.

The miracle is that I wasn't angry with myself for being _____ (fill in the blank with whatever was my negative self-talk): "I'm not enough: Too fat, too tired, hungry, too sore, uncomfortable and constipated. I did it wrong. It's always the money and the ever-dreaded... "they." If I don't like it I change it. Period. Whatever "it" is. I change it inside of me and let go of thinking it's somewhere else. This keeps showing up as miracles. Staying present and truly grateful fuels the manifesting beauty in my life today.

The miracle is that each hotel room is small, comfortable and affordable, equipped with everything I could ever need. The linens are new, fresh and clean. I was looking for greatness (and finding it) instead of only seeing the discomforts, contrasts and challenges possible in every single scenario. The miracle is: I have changed my point of view and the world has offered me a much better view to enjoy.

Consider that living in pain and agony, strife and difficulty, conflict and deficit could be a pattern. I did. I changed that pattern. After nearly 40 years, the pattern was broken, and the programs rewritten, by doing one main thing: I decided to! I made the decision to change once and for all by allowing myself to be exactly who I am and letting go of feeling negative about it. This keeps showing up in miracles.

Here is the momentous story of the miraculous trip in the language of love that manifested through Italy for my husband and I.

First stop: Rome. My husband of nearly 25 years, being Italian, was thrilled about this complimentary company trip for two he earned through diligent hard work. (Miracle? Maybe.) How about tacking on five extra nights and not freaking out about it? (Miracle? For sure!) Because he was so busy providing for the family, I took the reins and put together the details of our journey.

Using my instincts and following my well-honed street smarts that I learned while growing up moving from place to place with nearly nothing at all, I booked rooms and rides for our adventure. Putting aside with full respect the warnings of crime, thievery and plain old bad conditions, I kept my gaze steady on the outcomes I wanted. It was a far cry from being overwhelmed and insecure about what might go wrong. I held tightly to the picture of prosperity. I was curious to see what would go right!

We arrived to find...

The grand columns, *the massive stacked rock, and stone structures were astounding. They lay halfway intact just to the left of our gracious hotel.*

The ruins and grandeur, *the sheer size of the possible lifestyle of the ancient Romans left the imagination soaring. It was overwhelmingly expressed through steps and fountains, statues and astonishment. The huge openings to the underground city lay bare and revealing. We guessed where the ferocious animals and chariots entered into the arena of the Coliseum.*

The awe of the vast square named for St. Peter circled us for a view of collective thinking and prayers of the masses.

The vino—the grape—is the gift of this region. We poured over many a table wine, laughter and light hearts with dear friends, free to walk around and take advantage of a place built by millions of workers who lived before us thousands of years ago. I could imagine so many people walking the same steps.

Yes, the city of Rome has my heart. I have fallen in love.

The heart center asks for nothing but waits to be honored and nurtured to reveal its truth. Coming from the heart is a lifelong nurturing relationship. Listen well and listen only to what sounds and feels loving. The heart is not angry and vengeful. The heart is not weak. It may be soft-spoken and searching for its moment to safely appear. Find the language of your heart, its desires and tastes. Listen carefully to it. Feed your heart often and well. Go there. Live there. This is where true joy is to be found.

I come from loving-kindness.

Only 27 hours in a city, can it be true love? Love is a miracle. And so is finding our train to Venice.

Somehow, luck would have it; first class is where we landed. It includes drinks and snacks and comfortable seats, which keep us entertained over the next 3½-hour ride.

To be prepared I eat well, stretch often and rest fully every day.

Being Italian, my husband celebrates each and every day of the year. Slowly, I have learned it possible to do the same. For me, balance is key. Having my wits, knowing my whereabouts and radiating strong positive energy—that is what I celebrate. Especially when things can get lost in translation.

Our train stops. We journey into the city of bridges. We are "helped" with our bags for way too much euro. I am thankful. The short walk to our modest room on the quiet northeast side of the station was as simple as one could ask when you manifest with ease and grace.

We check in and find...

I'm thankful for the good fortune or miracle of finding our modest, well-priced, priceless room. Location and timing are everything. We have arrived.

The fantasy of Venice is captivating. The beauty is hypnotic. The waterways and mysterious lifestyle is mesmerizing, and the discovery of the familiar combined with the never-imagined charms my spirit.

We languish in the lifestyle of 007 while taking a ride down the Grand Canal in the Italian speedboat with tufted, caramel-colored leather seats.

It was that time of day in Italy where every shop takes a siesta at about 3 pm, except for, as luck would have it, the excellent little spot below our window. It so happened to be the place serving drink, food and live soothing music that comforted me late into the night.

I could hear George's laughter drift into my open-air window while I slipped in and out of sleep. Intertwined sounds of light jazzy rhythm and blues; forks, plates and glassware clinking lightly below gave me comfort.

The ancient wooden shutters on the two windows of our corner room were flung wide open and gave organic nostalgia to the vintage room. Gentle mosquitoes gathered in the corners of the ceiling and were late night entertainment while we laughed off having to take cover.

My God, I love Venice! I love the moment after moment after moment, each unfolding into a better one than the next. And I love that breakfast is included.

The sound of boats motoring by early in the day lets us awaken to a reality in Venice. Although I pledged my undying love to Rome only a day ago with my full heart, I do feel the guilty pleasure of a careless romantic weekend affair with Venice.

We leave our flat from the third floor, navigating to the train station as if we'd been there so many times before. We had walked the steps with so many—people, tourists, peddlers and locals—over and over again, living a Venetian fantasy. The masks, the gelato, the lemoncello and the espresso interlaced with the waterways, bridges, Murano glass and a tiny (grand) church that brought me to my knees in thanks and prayer.

This place will be cherished for its exciting thrill and mystery that will remain a secret kept, as it's truly indescribable. It was so good, part of me blushes when thinking of our treasured time here. The mosquitoes are forgiven.

I practice forgiveness.

In a mad dash to the train I blow a kiss to the sweet gondola and endless carafes of red. On the train we celebrate, we laugh, and we promise our love and dash away to the official agenda. The company trip begins by boarding the cruise ship in the port of Rome.

Because of a short delay there is a chance we will miss our connecting train, but we hurry. In the "fear" on my face and in my field, I attract a set of three gypsies. They are urgent. They are helpful. We run furiously to catch the train while the "helpers" start shuffling our bags, throwing them into the train and carrying them in what seems like many directions. The conductor yells, "Mind your bags!" with a great force locking eyes with me. My heart sinks.

Confusion mixed with urgency and the undiscovered pattern of "nearly missing the train" at play, we pay the fee insisted by the trio and I'm nervously thankful, dripping beads of sweat, to still have all of my belongings in sight. Nothing was lost. I continue to keep my wits about me while we rest into the train after a long night of mosquito hunting.

The momentum of travel, the rolling bags and rhythm of on and off the train lends to the momentum of learning. I lean into slowing my breath with clear and simplified thoughts. This slows my pulse and my racing heart. I watch my words for negatives and fears as this steps me backward in life.

Travel fatigue leads to mental clangor. I am aware. *Find the lesson*, I tell myself. *Find the forward-thinking words. Find truth. Use positives*. This brings momentum continuously forward.

The romance of Rome and the guilty pleasure of Venice nearly come to a halt with the stark contrast of the formality of our ship. Our travel mate appears with bright smiling eyes and an uncorked bottle in hand. Cups in tow, we pour into the taxi and ride onward toward the cruise. We sing with celebration to have manifested this trip.

Side note: Because of the drastic shift from the authentic, albeit touristy flavors, of Italy to the mostly American party on the ship, we had a great opportunity to compare and even complain. Please be aware that continuous momentum and manifestation and deep peace are in flow when staying focused and finding the gift in each and every event. The opposite creates an opposing force. Keep the mind and body steady and limber, able to move and be centered—flowing with what is.

Day One Aboard: *Our journey to Pisa wasn't scheduled. It was a reroute due to rough seas, weather and wind keeping us from the Isle of Capri. What* **is** *this Pisa anyway?*

Without letting disappointment take over I remember there could be something better in store. Be limber, flexible and open.

Letting go of expectation, I ask God to show me what I am to learn in this obvious detour to destiny by His design. My discovery: Charm.

Grandeur and charm live hand in hand. Charm. Pisa. Quaint. Roaming meandering streets, the thirty-five thousand students, and a subtle presence in the charming quaint town. My eyes are widened and my heart is warmed. I am enchanted. I feel the quality of Pisa, its struggle and its church. The leaning tower... it's so discrete. I love Pisa and all it has to offer. Funny it's known for the negative story of the leaning tower. A focus on a mistake turned into a magnificent monument of possibility. I look beyond the flaw.

We hang on every poignant syllable of our passionate, knowledgeable guide. We enter the grand church and are in pure awe of its 850-year construction. In the Baptistry of St. John, we listen to the acapella notes in the baptismal song swirling around us, suspended under the high, rounded ceiling once open to rainfall, for the purpose of baptism. Heart-opening vibrant notes, beauty and golden grace, this domed roof, so close to heaven, welcoming new souls entering (as I am) into La Vita Nuova, *the new life. I can say so much about Pisa and somehow, feel I can say nothing. It is so very captivating. I am charmed by Pisa like a long, sweet stolen kiss.*

Next stop*: Florence.*

In my mind, I do my best not to jump forward, knowing about the ten-hour touristy tour ahead, plus five hours more after that. It can feel exhausting, so I stay in present time where it is safe and sound.

We are well provided for: Room service and an attentive staff. Florence provides David, Michael Angelo, Di Vinci's work and the story of mother, father and son. It's a strict town. Going from group to group and room-to-room full of paintings and statuary is dizzying. Our lunch: A prize atop a rooftop room overlooking the great church. Sparkling wine and Chianti Classico midday—we feel like royalty and set out for more to see.

For me, Florence is a vast place filled with a history of control and order. For me, this day in a town I barely know, it's all business to keep up with the 10-hour foot tour. In this little snapshot of Firenze, I know so little. In full and deep gratitude for all that is here and all that it came from, I say to Florence, "It was nice to see you. Let's do lunch."

And so we go. More movement—more momentum; keeping my gaze strong. When I think of what we experience as we manifest all that we have, I consider my options. I consider my choices. Our nightlife influences our mornings again and the early day unfolds this time in France. For this tiny trip, I know not what to expect. I do know that expectation can dampen the best of intentions. I let go of expectation and open my eyes and my heart. I find myself still filled with love for Rome and the temptation of Venice, with the sweetness of Pisa and wisdom of Florence. Now, with childlike eyes, I wonder, what will the day in France bring?

I create my reality.

It is from my heart that I live. Both a skill and a restful place, from which I travel, content and awakened. It is listening from deep within that guides my way. It's the Light with which I connect. The Lightness of joy and laughter I cultivate on purpose. I've chosen to learn this... this time around. I allow the Light to illuminate my path as I mindfully take each step. I pause and wait patiently for the notes, sounds and songs to guide my way.

We arrive at St. Paul-de-Vence. The romance inside the walled city is something I could have never dreamt of in my wildest French dreams. I have no reference. This is so brand new to me: A French colony of artists.

The sweet nurturing of the French cottage chapel fronting the ancient colony takes me in at first glance. The walled ancient city... protective, unassuming, and revealing treasures of every shape, size, color and concept. My mouth is wide open. My eyes sparkle with surprise. The scent of lavender, the weight of glass, bronze and gold adorning walls, steps and staircases in colors that tickle my senses. It is so beautiful here.

We only met there for a short time in France. Finishing with a small rosé and crepe. It was all we had time for. St. Paul-de-Vence, a short detour from my Italian love escapade, captured my attention like an unexpected proposal to run away together and elope. I felt flattered, awakened and seen through an eccentric artist's caring eye. As I waved goodbye to the opulent possibilities of Monaco and France, I knew I was nearly swept off my feet. Au revoir, Mon'Amie. I know we may never meet again . . .

Staying fully present, well and in good form is a conscious choice I made for myself a long time ago... in 1994. It was my decision to be well, pain-free and energized, naturally happy and whole—that's my mission. I confirm this choice often. I teach others the same. Today, I am thankful and remind myself of my bigger mission. My decision keeps a passionate, positive momentum in reach at all times. I pause. I take a moment to see, feel and smell the miracle that could be happening in my life now.

Momentum is movement from accumulated actions. Momentum is a flow that we step into, consciously or otherwise. The gifts that manifest can be called miracles... miracles of every single day of life.

The next miracle I encounter is safe delivery from the shores of Monaco to the large ship, in the dangerously high, wild seas of this spring day. Many faces are grey and green around the gills. Many eyes are wide and heavy on the small tender (water taxi) but I set my gaze within; I share my inner light by wishing each and every person well and safe.

Aware of the magnificent and powerful blue waters, I am but a speck. Unknowing what lies ahead is the precise place where faith is found.

The gift of the unknown can feel like a curse when the mind is untamed. Oh, so deftly, the past casts shadows over possibilities here in the moment when we are in the habit of believing old references. The future, a place of unknowing. Choose a vision. Connect with it. Know.

Let go of the old stories by creating new ones in the moment of the unknown. Manifesting is possible—it's happening now. Using positive momentum and the clarity of stillness, one cultivates *on purpose* through observation, patience and practice. Be still. Be patient. Observe.

Feeling the tides of days, nights, flights, trains, travels, cheers, jams and jubilations, the final day at sea has arrived. A crossroads: What to do on the last excursion ashore? Rest or carry on? Rough seas and rain had colored two of our days, leaving us perfectly content with a bit of a slower pace.

Peeling my eyelids open for an early day gave way to reconfirmation of an intention I set so long ago. It is my intention to feel well, energized and able to live a rich, full exploration of this life. I had done the opposite in the first half of my life. Today I carry on.

For happiness, health and vitality, I live my truth.

Without a glance backward, I dress in a fresh Ralph Lauren polka dot, swing dress and travel ashore to the small port of Portofino—a miracle in and of it's self. Motoring into the small seaport fishing village calms my heart and awakens awe in the magnificence this cove.

The beauty here humbles me. Being alive and well rewards me. I am aware of this and deeply thankful for the

96

miracle of Portofino. We walk the long, winding, quiet path up the old lane to the church. The grand homes nestle quietly into the landscape overlooking the magical water's edge. It centers me, fills me and understands me. Being here in Portofino is like being with my lifelong, best friend.

Today I am comfortable, happy, unconditionally loved and ask for nothing in return. Somehow, I know I'm safe. I feel like more of "me" here; more myself. A place I could rest in for hours or days or forever... a place to dine or drink cappuccino or indulge on gelato parfait, just because.

This day a miracle has shown itself through the calm completion of our company trip. Portofino feels a deep calm yin to the vast yang of Venice. The color of the sun and glistening deep azure blue is a miracle of nature and so is my easily walking those thousand steps toward the positive generous life force it took to get here.

Just to be clear, there are many opportunities to "join the conversation" with tempting negative babble. It's true—misery loves company. What we focus on expands. Boo-hoo... wah wah... and never enough!. It's easy to get caught there. This I navigate through. I have been there before and walk past the opportunity to join in again. I choose Light, life-filled unconditional love. Portofino is my friend, whom I can't wait to see, and will often meet with again.

Thinking we are done with excursions brings a sigh of relief while we travel across the ripples of blue-gold to get back aboard the floating hotel. I was wrong. There returns the urgency to pack, dress and hasten to the final affair of the business portion of our trip, which brings another opportunity to center, stay grounded and show up alive and well. It can be a challenge.

I can let action, pace and indigestion get the best of me. I can give up and not show up in the end. I can complain, become a drain and contaminate the luxurious space. Or... I can let go of the negatives, stay deeply grateful and authentically positive (which brings energy), and complete my journey of a lifetime.

And so it goes. Elegant casual is the dress code for the farewell poolside affair at sunset. I excuse myself a moment early feeling neither elegant nor casual and just want rest.

Disembarking this morning and leaving the crowd hedges a slight feeling of intimidation. It's like being set out on your own in life without a chaperone to guide the way. It's just my husband and I and we opt to drag our bags to find our next train. We second-guess this choice in the end. Only two more nights and we will return home. We can do this.

My thought is "follow through." I'd made the plans with childhood friends so, Salerno, here we come. Gladly, we head for the land of unknown with the reputation of the Amalfi Coast. We are tired, we are excited and we are greeted with open arms. This time the train has no frills, no thrills and not much to eat. Thankful for the peddler with his pail of bread, sandwiches and wine. Gluten-free is a thing in the States, but here I eat gladly.

With friends that feel like family, we are happy to arrive. We stroll through the villages, walk the streets, talk with the locals, understanding only hand signals and the glistening love coming from their eyes. We carry on deep into the night, walking and shopping and chatting and sharing. We see ceramics. We see lemon terraces. We see a sunset view worth a million euro or more. How can we go much further without food or drink this late in the night?

When visiting the home of a family or friend, manners are in play. The endless buffets of the cruise are long gone. The street side cafés of the cities are far off. The hunger and thirst grow as the insistent groans in my tummy increase. I can feel my eyes opening wider and wider as my adrenals take the lead. Survival! But, alas, we are with family and all is well. Joining the table for an unexpected 7-course meal at 8:45 pm with full authentic Italian flair, I am safe, I am tired and I am FULL. And it's 1 AM.

I write this trip of momentum, miracles and manifestation as I have lived it in more glory than anything ever traveled in life before, because I sit still looking out the window of this train (that we nearly missed) to get to the connector in time for the layover at the airport before another 17 hours of travel home. I still choose happiness.

I am home here, as I am in my heart, my mind and my body all at once. I have nowhere to be, nothing to wish for, I am fully content in the moment now. Where I live is where I take care of myself. I can only do my best.

The work in writing is in the sharing of my journey to inner peace manifested after years and years (and more years) of pain, suffering and strife. The pain is no longer my story. My story is one to be written. My story is positively divine and beautifully abundant. I'm here to help others live the beautiful life they came to live and may not think possible. I'm here to be sure my energy is strong, my body is agile and my voice is clear in each moment. That's all I can do. This is what I choose. I take care of my vessel for the highest good, in order to teach the skill of manifestation, witnessing miracles and staying in the flowing momentum of positive forward movement... found even in stillness.

I feel like this next leg home will bring me to a new place in my life. I feel as if I have traveled a lifetime and come forward anew. There is a higher sense of joy that comes home with me. Joy a lifetime deep. I came home a woman knowing a new man and where he comes from. I came home knowing a new family, seeing the traditions alive and living.

I came home with not only a happy man, but also one who makes joy from flour, water and salt. His joy of fishing comes from a deep long relationship with the sea. The wealth of living along the impossible cliffs is shown in the scent of sweet tangy lemon; lemon juice, lemon cake and lemoncello. Where everything is possible. I have a husband whose family built villages, castles, churches and works of art along cliffs, water cities and impossible coves. I know more than ever before: He can do anything. And he now knows what I newly know of myself... we can do anything, together.

I come home with a new relationship, not just sharing the romance of a vacation away but now with a new sense of respect... he for me; I for him. He looks at me, knowing I capably took him to the kneecap of the boot-shaped country to which his heritage belongs. Maybe, to his surprise, I showed up with grace and ease—gracefully, easily. He got me from train to train and shore to shore with strength and delight. I got him from room to room and table to table.

We grew this journey together. We come home refreshed, having walked through a lifelong love affair with Italy.

My heart is devoutly in love, and devoted to Rome, a short tryst in Venice, a stolen kiss with Pisa, nearly running away with France and resting comfortably with the best friend of Portofino – Salerno. A visit with family sends me home. Happy, sound, and safe... I call this journey a miracle. I am grateful. I am blessed.

In manifesting; we create our reality.

Another story could have been filled with accents of scratchy throats, long days, blistered feet, fear of missing the boat, the plane, the cruise, the blasted train. It could have focused on seasickness, being tired, no vegetables in sight. It could have been a recounting of dairy intolerance, gluten indulgence, bloating, and constipation that accompanies every trip. It could have been flavored with the fatigue of travel, the long flight home, and the fact that I had to "do it all" and could never rest. Not a fun or flavorful story. What story do you tell?

Energy follows thought.

What we focus on expands. What are you focused on, now? How will you strengthen your gaze? Into those foreign experiences we go, wondering what miracles await us. Or do we choose to create those miracles ourselves in each moment?

Ciao for now. With love...

Valerie

About the Author

VALERIE'S PASSION IS teaching others "The Simple Art of Manifesting," remaining in the moment, staying centered, grounded and learning to receive and create in flow with change and growth. It is her mission is to open the passageway for the spiritual homemaker living a traditional yet not so traditional life.

She is a transformational teacher, speaker, author and workshop host. As a healer and a deep listener, Valerie has traveled the world to learn with master teachers the art of creating spiritually infused space to thrive in within you and around you. Valerie uses Advanced Vision Board processes to easily and quickly transform from the basic foundations of manifesting. Her gift is to hold the space for true growth, positive change and the discovery of your soft power. She holds retreats in remote places in the world for the nurturing of inner peace, as well as teaching teleclasses on how to simplify live into happiness.

The mother of two, happily married for over 25 years, a daughter, a wife and a yogi, Valerie helps those who are looking for the gentle understandings of this existence and believes that the peace we seek is found within and reflected in everything we see. Valerie has made a change; by making a choice, she has healed. She chose a positively, rich and wonderful life filled with abundance, grace, ease, momentum, miracles and manifestation.

You can always connect here:

Life Energy Coach
http://foundationsofmanifesting.com
Valerie@LifeEnergyCoach.com
www.valsgift.com
http://www.amazon.com/Valerie-Sorrentino/e/B00IB5HCRU

Chapter 6

I M POSSIBLE

Angie Toh

Do you choose Impossible or I'm Possible?

I prefer to believe that we live in a world of possibilities where miracles can and will happen if we believe and allow.

~ Angie Toh

Introduction

DO YOU BELIEVE in manifestation and miracles? Do you believe that we live in a world of possibilities? If you would have asked me these questions fifteen years ago I would have given you a strong, convicted "No" as my answer! My life prior to doing any kind of personal development work was one filled with limitations; limitations not from other people, but from me.

I was a senior prison officer after graduating from University, and just like the inmates that I met everyday, I built a high wall and became a prisoner of my own life. The inmates I met in my work lived in a physical prison with high walls; I lived in a prison with invisible high walls that I built for myself. I locked the doors and I held the keys to those doors. I was living a life by autopilot, unfulfilled and unhappy and I never trusted people enough to allow them in my life. I did not know how to love myself and needless to say, I did not know how to love others. I lived a mediocre life... I played small and made myself invisible.

In 2005 at age 35, I hit rock bottom. I was jobless, having quit my job in 2004 to start a business venture with friends. The business had not generated any money after a full year and I left feeling disillusioned with others and myself – not to mention being financially devastated. I tried applying for job but was told at 35 I was too old. To make matter worse, I had to go through a major surgery during that time and had barely recovered from the surgery.

When "Not Good Enough" is Your Mantra

AT WHAT MAY have been one of the lowest points of my life, that lowest point, I responded to a newspaper advertisement to attend a free seminar; which became a turning point in my life. During that two-hour seminar, I heard the speaker talking about success, abundance, and how to make money with little or no money. Listening to her gave me gave me some light in the pitch-dark place that I had been in for the last few months. On that important day in October 2005, I used my credit card to fund my very first personal development and growth journey; an inner journey within that was offering me a life I never thought possible.

In addition to attending workshops and seminars, I was also introduced to Breathwork, a conscious connected breathing technique that in 2006 had been around for more than 40 years. This safe and powerful technique is used to help release suppressed emotions, birth trauma, limiting thought patterns, stress and tension. Through the many private breathwork sessions I had with my Breathworker I was able to release many disempowering belief and thought patterns. I came to realize that the first thought I too frequently allowed myself to have in life was, " I'm not good enough." Too many negative feelings flooded my being... "Yes, I am not good enough since my parents wanted a baby boy and I am a girl."

Understanding gave me recognition that with this limiting belief, it was no wonder I always ran away just when success was within reach. I began to understand why I was so afraid of success and how I sabotaged myself whenever I was doing well in my career. The unconscious belief of "not good enough" was running my life and that I was also struggling a lot with my own femininity—feeling myself "not good enough" as a girl.

The next six years were filled with transformation brought through breathwork, coaching and many personal-development training programs. From the ashes of a woman with low self esteem and diminished confidence came the fires of a powerful woman with

107

strength, faith and a belief in the IM-Possible. Life had never felt this great and I thought that all my challenges in life were over. I was holding an ideal dream job in a global coaching organization; I had the privilege to travel and was making more money that I ever had made. Never did I expect to go through another intense year. However, in 2011 I was challenged by more tests from the Universe. I guess the experiences that I went through in 2011 were big tests to see how much I would put into practice what I learned during the previous the years. The test: *Have I integrated what I learned over the last six years or was it all merely knowledge that I accumulated?*

The Hysterectomy

IN THE FIRST week of January in 2011, I finally dragged myself to see my gynecologist; the pain was becoming almost unbearable. I was experiencing intense debilitating pain every day, no longer just during my menstrual cycle. Daily doses of painkillers no longer worked for me despite the fact that I was on a high dosage prescription. For the last 10 years, I had been living with adenomyosis and endometriosis. Despite two earlier surgeries and many other conventional and alternative treatments, my conditions had not improved. Previously, my gynecologist had been focusing on saving my uterus, since I was still single and still hoping to have a family one day.

This time around, however, the recommendation from the gynecologist was clear: I needed a hysterectomy. There was no way to save my uterus as it was badly inflamed and the blood cysts were in the muscles of the uterus. I remembered leaving the clinic feeling low and depressed. *For years I have been battling with my own feminine issue, and the thought of living the next phase of my life without a uterus is not something I am prepared to deal with. Will I still be a woman without a uterus? Will any man want to marry a woman without a uterus?* It took me more than a month of deep work and processes to heal the emotional pain, but by the time the surgery was scheduled in the first week of March, I was feeling at peace and ready to embrace my new found femininity without a uterus.

Instead of open surgery, new technology allowed the hysterectomy to be done via a keyhole surgery. I had experienced open surgery before in 2005 and remember feeling, *I am so glad that this time round, I need not go through the intense pain of an open surgery and should be able to recovered fully within two to four weeks.* These were my thoughts until I was fully conscious following the surgery. My surgeon came to my bedside and told me that he ruptured a hole in my bladder during the surgery. Though the hole was stitched up, I would need to be on a catheter for at least a week to allow my bladder to heal. Though I was not too happy to be hooked to a catheter for a week, I adjusted and learned to live with a special bag that was strapped to my ankle 24/7, and thankfully discharged from the hospital within two days of the surgery.

Many friends asked me why I didn't take legal action with the surgeon since he raptured my bladder. In my own thoughts, I was more focused on my recovery and deep down, I knew it was more of a complication from the surgery rather than a physician's negligence and there was no valid reason to hold him accountable for the injury.

Giving all my focus to healing, I recovered quickly and was able to remove the catheter within a week after the surgery and quietly thought, *Now, I am ready for my new life!*

I enrolled to attend a seminar the following week and was so eager to be out to meet people and start my new life. The day right after the weekend seminar I realized that there was a recurrence of bleeding, and I was leaking urine constantly. I went straight to the hospital and was told that the bladder wound has ruptured and was inflamed. Once again, I was hooked to a catheter and referred to an urologist since the extent of this complication was beyond what my gynecologist could manage. The prognosis by the urologist was not good. Most likely I would need another surgery to fix the rupture. However, he suggested once again connecting me to a catheter for the next few weeks and seeing how the healing would progress. Obviously, I was devastated when I first heard the news. *Why me? Why do I have to go through this again?*

Manifesting Miracles

SOME SOLACE WAS found when my mentor suggested that when things happen, instead of asking, "Why me," I should ask, "Why not me?" Though it was difficult to live a quality life with a catheter attached, I decided not to let this experience affect me. *I want to put all my focus on manifesting a miracle instead of allowing myself to be a victim of this situation. I want to allow the rupture in my bladder to heal completely without having to go through any more surgery.*

I talked to my bladder, I prayed, I visualized the ideal outcome I liked to see what transpired as I worked on keeping my spirits high. I stayed home most of the time and only stepped out of the house when I absolutely needed to. Oh, the inconvenience of walking around with a urine bag!

Fortunately, I was able to resume work as I could work from home. I also bought myself nice sexy, long dresses to wear to hide the urine bag whenever I need to be out of the house.

Six weeks was the time frame the urologist had given me to see whether I could recover fully without the need for a surgery. Every appointment date with him was nerve wrecking; I could never be sure what is going to happen next. I put all my heart and soul into focusing on the miracle I wanted.

In the first week of May, after six weeks of a close relationship with catheter and walking around with my urine bag, I was given the best birthday present ever. The bladder had healed perfectly and the urologist was able to remove what had become my closest friend! The miracle that I had focused on creating had manifested right before me. I was able to function normally without a catheter and there was no need for another surgery.

Reflecting back on that time, I realize that was probably my first experience of using mind power for healing. I have always believed in the power of our mind and how our mind and emotions can affect our healing and through this life challenge I got to experience first hand how it actually works. Physically, I was still weak from the surgery and the complications. You can well imagine, however, emotionally I was feeling great. In fact, I was feeling rather "over the moon" with the miracle of not having to go through any more surgery and able to have a healthy functioning bladder again.

In June, I decided to enroll in a gym and engage a personal trainer to help me to work on improving my stamina. I started working out about three times a week and was really feeling at the peak of my life. I felt more feminine than ever, I felt sexy, I felt powerful and embraced that I had a successful career. I possessed a pain free body after dealing with pain almost everyday for more than 10 years. Everything seemed to be working well again in my life.

Unfortunately, I was also getting a little preoccupied and focusing more on my outer world rather than my inner being. I experienced the feelings of being impatient with people who were less successful than me. The recognition set in... *I am out of touch with divine love, constantly Doing instead of Being, wanting to achieve more and more and refusing to slow down. I am getting very impatient and want things to happen the way I want them.* I forgot all about meditation... or prayers... or to be in touch with my higher self. I was consumed with the need to look good and to buy back the lost time that I had in the first half of the year.

When we stop listening to our inner voices, sometime God has to send us a big truck to knock us over so as to make us listen once again! That was precisely what He did, barely two months after my full recovery from the hysterectomy and the complications.

The Freak Fall

ON 22 JULY, I was in Carpenter Street for an appointment in the morning as a model for a beauty college student doing her manicure exam. I said yes to being a model, not because I wanted to be of help and service to the student and supporting her, but thinking. *Since I need a manicure, why not save some money and have a gel manicure done?* I remember feeling very uptight and impatient the whole morning but I was not listening to my inner voice or intuition. I had my nails done up beautifully and was ready to move to my next appointment. While stepping out of the lift carrying my laptop and other stuff in my shoulder bag, I missed one very small step and lost my balance. However, instead of falling down, I kept moving forward for another 1m before falling off a 50cm height from the walkway to the road.

I landed sitting on the road, immediately feeling a sharp pain in my right shoulder and not able to move my right arm. A few staff members from a shop witnessing the whole incident came forward to help me. I was brought into the shop and waited for my friend to come and pick me up. Initially, I thought I might just have a minor injury, probably tearing some muscle of my shoulder, and was not planning to go to the hospital. However, the pain did get more intense and I was advised to go to the hospital for an x-ray.

While lying in the Accident and Emergency area of the hospital waiting for my x-ray results, I was praying and hoping that I did not break any bones and would be able to recovery quickly. I was told that I broken and dislocated my right humerus head. Barely two months after

113

recovering from my first surgery, I found myself once again on an operation table, and this time round to deal with a bigger test, the possibility of never gaining full function of my dormant arm again. Just the day before, I was in the gym carrying weights and running around, yet in a split second I had potentially lost all function of my right arm. Once again, *"Why me"? Why do I have to deal with yet another trial in my life so soon again?*

The surgeon inserted a stainless steel plate and nine screws to hold my humerus head together. This was the fifth surgery that I had undergone over a period of 11 years and the second one in 2011. Sorrowfully, it was by far the most painful surgery that I ever experienced; the pain after the anesthesia went off was excruciating. I was constantly begging for painkillers and nothing that I attempted to do could distract me from the pain. *I am one person that sleeps easily and yet for the first time in my life, I am experiencing countless night of insomnia, and this pain is just too intense for me to sleep.*

Without my dormant arm, I felt so helpless, needing a helper to assist me with my shower, to dress and undress me and even to help me to comb my hair. And I was struggling to do even basic activities like eating and brushing my teeth with my left arm. *Why is it that all the activities I found so easy and taken for granted now seem so impossible?*

My right arm was glued to my side and I had limited range of movement even three months after the surgery. I was told by my surgeon that this was a serious injury and I would never able again have full function of my right arm, forcing me to accept that I would live with limitations of

114

my right arm for the rest of my life. Every physiotherapy sessions were painful and despite my continued efforts, I was not seeing any significant improvement. *I am beginning to buy in to the power of my surgeon words... maybe I will never fully recover and I will be living with limitations for the rest of my life.*

Once again, I told myself, I need to focus on the impossible. I need to create another miracle and not buy in to the verdict of my surgeon. I need to visualize the ideal outcome that I want, a complete recovery of my arm. With these thoughts in mind I fired the physiotherapists from the hospital and found a good therapist in private practice; I built a team of people to support me in this new healing journey. Together with my physiotherapist, massage therapist, personal trainer, my spiritual guides and angels, we worked on creating the full recovery I envisioned in my mind.

Slowly but surely, I began to make some progress, celebrating every small achievement along the way; even if was just to be able to move my arm higher by an inch. I was like a baby learning how to use my right arm to execute simple activities that I used to take for granted. *Well, how difficult is it to hold a spoon and put food in your mouth, to brush your teeth or even just to comb your hair? I used to be able to perform those activities without blinking an eyelid and never in my wildest dreams would I expect that I would have to struggle and relearn to do them all over again.*

This long road to recovery was not an easy one but I never once gave up the belief that I would recover fully. Whenever my doctor reminded me that I was going to

115

have limitations, I told him with conviction, "No, I will not!"

Over the next three months, I gained back 60% of my arm function and within a year after the surgery, my arm was as good as new. No one could tell that I had a serious injury except for the long scar on my arm. I could do boxing, carry weights in the gym, and be confident my arm was much stronger compared to many people out there. What was deemed impossible in the eye of a medical professional is now my reality!

Do Not Give Your Power Away

"Don't let someone tell you that you can't do something.
Not even me.
You got a dream. You gotta protect it. When people can't do something themselves, they're gonna tell you that you can't do it.
If you want something, go get it. Period."

~ Will Smith in The Pursuit of Happiness

YOU GIVE YOUR power away when you make someone outside of you more important than what you hold inside of yourself. It is easy for us to give our power away, especially to the so call "experts." We will give our power away to doctors, therapists, coaches, spiritual masters, astrologists, etc. In reality, however, we are the masters of our own life. No one knows us as well as we know ourselves. No one has the right to take our power away, and nor should we give our power away. We become a victim the moment we give our power away.

I was able to recover so quickly and completely because I chose **not** to give my power to my surgeon. He might have done a great job repairing my bones and I'm truly grateful to him for that. However, he cannot play God or tell me how much I can recover. If I had listened to his words and believed that it was all right to live with limitations of my arm, I would probably never have the use of it with which I am blessed today.

Other than giving our power away to experts, we may also give our personal power to our partners, friends, an unfulfilling job, or to our fear and insecurities. Own your personal power today, you are the director of your own life-movie and no one other than you can or should determine how that script should be written.

Believe in the Possibilities

"Man often becomes what he believes himself to be. If I keep on saying to myself that I cannot do a certain thing, it is possible that I may end by really becoming incapable of doing it. On the contrary, if I have the belief that I can do it, I shall surely acquire the capacity to do it even if I may not have it at the beginning."
~ Mahatma Gandhi

AS FAR BACK as 2005 my mentor taught me we live in a world of possibilities and miracles do happen everyday, if only we allow. Thus, no matter what challenges I faced in my life, I never again allowed myself to entertain any thoughts of impossibilities. Instead of focusing on what is not possible, if I really want something in life and is in alignment with my values, I will ask myself, "How can I

117

make it possible, what will it take to create the possibilities?"

Other than the healing I experienced in 2011, the same mindset has also helped me to create many other positive changes I wanted in my life, one of which was to rid myself of a deep fear of speaking in public. Public speaking used to be my number one fear in life! *I dare not ask questions in class and I* **will** *run away from any opportunity to speak in front of anyone, even if is just to people; that is enough to make me tremble with fear and anxiety.* You would easily recognize me... I'm the one that would rather be lying in the coffin than standing up to give a eulogy. Limiting beliefs like: "My English is not good enough," "I cannot express myself well," "I don't have any energy," "I don't want to be in the limelight," and "I don't like to talk" would be in my head whenever someone merely suggested that I could explore becoming a teacher or trainer.

Never in my wildest dream would I have imagined that I could become a full time trainer, speaker and coach one day! And then came that most auspicious day in 2008 when I boldly told myself, "Enough is enough! It is time to work on releasing the fear of public speaking and allow my voice to be heard." Strangely, speaking opportunities started coming to me after I made that commitment to release my fear. The first training that I delivered in 2009 was nerve wracking for me, but I survived and don't think any of the participants would have known that it was my "virgin" public talk.

It gets easier as I continue to work on my releasing my own limiting beliefs and being open to more practice and experience. I would have told you prior to 2008 that it was impossible for me to ever give a public talk, but now what was once impossible is now almost a daily affair.

Remember, nothing is impossible when we embrace our "big why" and commit to the determination to see it through. What is one thing that you would like to have or do in your life and yet the thought of impossibility had stopped you from moving forward? *I pray my readers will be inspired after reading my story to step up and own their power and make the impossible possible!*

Miracles Can Happen to Anyone

"There are only two ways to live your life. One is as though nothing is a miracle. The other is as though everything is a miracle."

~ Albert Einstein

AFTER READING THIS some of you might find an inner voice telling you, "All the stories she shared could only happen to her, it cannot happen to me!" You might be like the person I used to be, sitting on the fence and thinking miracles can and only will happen to other people instead of you. That was exactly how I felt when one of the instructors of my first personal development training shared how he was broke with no money and wanted so badly to attend an important training call, *Money and You.* Somehow, he managed to secure a loan to fund his training—even though he was then on the verge of filing for a bankruptcy. I vividly remember sitting in the audience seat and thinking, *such miracles can only happen to you... never to me. I still have no money and my credit*

119

card has been maxed out, there is no way that I can afford this training. Is not meant for me.

At the end of the training that night... after all the sharing on miracles and possibilities, one of my course mates, Roberto, came to me and asked "Angie, would you like to attend this *Money and You* training? Somehow I know your financial situation right now and I don't know why I am doing this, but I want you to know that if you like to attend the training, I can offer to pay for you first, and you can pay me back when you have earned the money." I was almost in tears when I heard that offer. *A while ago, here I was sitting there thinking that miracles can only happen to other people but not me, and now this person, whom I barely met five-weeks ago is making an offer to loan me money to attend this training.*

Yes, I accepted his offer and attended the *Money and You* training in 2005. It was one major turning point in my life. In this program, I learned that for things in my life to change, first I must change. I learned to take responsibility for my own thoughts and feelings and to start "creating" a new life. I started to create income right after the training and within a year after completing the training, paid back my course mate – who is now a dear friend of mine.

Remember, miracles happen everyday and to everyone. You need first to believe and open your heart to receive.

Be Clear About What You Want to Manifest

Anything that you can imagine is yours to be or do or have. As you ask yourself why you want it, the essence of your desire is activated, and the Universe begins to bring it to you.
The more intense your positive feelings, the faster it is coming to you.
(It is as easy to create a castle as a button.)

~Abraham-Hicks

THOUGHTS ARE POWERFUL. What we focus on expands. We create our reality based on our thoughts. If we want to manifest something in our life, we need to be crystal clear with how we want that to happen, particularly the outcome we want.

I was supposed to attend a leadership meeting in Sydney, Australia, in July, 2011. Deep down, I didn't want to schedule this trip. First that is winter in Sydney. Born in a tropical country like Singapore, I am really not good dealing with cold weather. Moreover, how could I look good wrapping myself in those many layers of clothing? *I know I won't enjoy spending three days sitting in a room listening to endless reports of accomplishment and future plans, I like to act and get things done. This meeting just doesn't offer the hope of much excitement.*

Knowing not attending the meeting wasn't option since I was representing the Asia management team, I faithfully booked my air ticket and other accommodations. However, I remember telling a few friends 'How I wish I didn't have to go on this trip." I also remember thinking, "Unless I am really sick or end up in hospital, there is no

121

choice for me not to go to Sydney for the meeting." I did manifest what I wanted… not having to go for the meeting. Remember my horrible fall? It happened just five days before I was scheduled to travel to Sydney. However, it was definitely not the way I had wanted it to be. I would rather be in Sydney than lying in hospital with a broken arm and suffering in pain.

Reflecting back, I was not very clear with my manifestation. I know I didn't want to go for the trip; however, I was not specific how that could happen. I did not realize how powerful my thoughts could be, or how even those brief moment of passing thoughts to be physically unwell could become my reality.

I remembered praying and crying out "God, I did ask not to go for the trip but .you could create some minor illness like fever, chicken pox, etc. – why a freak accident that almost killed me and took me a year to recover?" I could almost see God looking into my eyes and said "Child, you said you didn't want to go for the trip and you get what you want, you did list staying in hospital as an option to be excused from this trip, however, you didn't state the reason to get you in hospital right? " Oh, right! I did not have intentions for what I want to call in, so I manifested what I didn't want, even though I did get the wish of not going for the trip. In hindsight, I learned not to use something negative as part of my manifestation.

I have learned to focus on what I want rather than what I do not want. I have learned to create a transparently clear image of the outcome I want. I have also learned to immediately cancel disempowering thoughts, knowing just how powerful my thoughts can be.

What is it in your life that you want to manifest? Is it a dream job, a dream house, a partner? Focus on what you desire, make a list, and be crystal clear on what you desire. Dream big and access the feeling of how you will feel when you manifest what you have stated in the list. Also, become an enlightened detective of your own thoughts. The moment you catch yourself having negative or disempowering thoughts, cancel them thoughts and replace your attention with empowering ones.

Maintain an Attitude of Gratitude

*Develop an attitude of gratitude, and give thanks for
everything that happens to you,
knowing that every step forward is a step
toward achieving something
bigger and better than your current situation.*
~ Brian Tracy

PRIOR TO THE incidents in 2011, I used to take my body for granted, I am not super fit but at least it is functionally properly, I can move my arms and carry stuff, I can walk, I can run, I can breathe. When I injured my arm, I thought, *fine, my right arm is injured but I still have both my legs and maybe I can still run.* However, just simply walking when your arm is in pain is already a challenge; running was not an option at all while I was recovering from the injury. I realized how our body parts are all inter-connected. I realized that I cannot take my body for granted. I learned to give thanks to my body parts everyday and learn to take good care of this physical body. My body is a vessel for me to contribute and serve in this world.

Let's agree to be grateful that we are alive today and have a body that can do what we need it to do for us. Let's also agree to be grateful for every experience that comes our way. Everything happens for a reason and we are never given more than what we can handle. Every experience that we have is intended either for us to grow and learn, or for us to thoroughly enjoy. Take a moment every morning and evening to give gratitude for the experiences that you have encountered throughout the day. Although it sounds cliché', there is much merit to the reality that, "An attitude of gratitude will accelerate your progress in life and bring you more joy!"

Endings and Beginnings

AFTER MY FULL recovery in 2012, I decided to quit my full time job to focus on my passion of helping others in their transformation. The long scar on my right shoulder is a daily reminder to me to be in the moment, to stay connected to my higher self, to love others, and myself and never to get carried away with a primary focus on success and money.

I am an ordinary woman that has managed to overcome many odds in my life and create an EXTRAordinary life. Like me, I know you too can create the extraordinary life that you design specially for yourself. Focus on creating the changes from within... deep lasting changes can only happen from the inside out, not from the outside in.

You are not limited by your race, age, sex, religion, birth country, lack of money or education. You are limited by your crippling fear, your doubts, your limiting beliefs, disempowering habits, your inner critic and your inability to take actions.
~ Angie Toh

About the Author

ANGIE TOH IS a peak performance and transformation coach and trainer. She is also the founder of iTransform, an institute for busy executives and business owners to create sustainable changes from within.

With her strong background in business, sales and marketing, Angie's passion is to help busy professionals and business owners **to *succeed at their own terms and achieve major breakthroughs in their personal and professional life***. Her mission in life is to facilitate and help others to gain insight into their true potential, to expand their awareness of who they could become as a person and live a purposeful and successful life. Her work is based on the concept that " For things to change, first I must change." Change can only be created when every person take 100% responsibility of their own thoughts, emotions and actions and work on their inner world using powerful tools like coaching, neuroscience, enneagram and breathwork.

Like the iceberg, our results in life and our behaviors are visible, while feelings and thoughts are hidden below the water. Many organizations and individuals are busy changing their visible results and behaviors instead of working on the invisible part of the iceberg; the emotions and thinking.

Certifications with which Angie has been accredited include: Results Coaching, Team Coaching, Money Coaching, Enneagram, Conscious Connected breathing breathwork, and Akashic Records Consultant.

Angie is one of the pioneer Breathworkers in Asia. Breathwork is a safe and powerful releasing technique that was developed in the early 70s to help release stress, suppressed emotions and limiting beliefs. It was through Breathwork that Angie was able to transform from a girl with low self esteem and fear of public speaking to who she is today, an international coach and speaker. Angie was featured on Channel News Asia AM Live program on 6 February 2012 sharing on the Power of the Breath.

Angie can be reached at:

https://www.facebook.com/angietoh
http://angietoh.com/
http://sg.linkedin.com/in/angietoh

Chapter 7

THE POWER OF PRAYER, SELF-LOVE, AND INTENTION… THE KEYS TO MANIFESTING AND CREATING MIRACLES IN YOUR LIFE

Jacqueline Van Campen

When your level of determination begins to change, everything else will begin to move in the direction you desire. The moment you resolve to be victorious, every nerve and fiber in your being will immediately orient itself toward your success. On the other hand, if you think, 'This is never going to work out,' then at that instant every cell in your being will be deflated and give up the fight, and then everything really will move in the direction of failure."

~ Daisaku Ikeda

LOOKING AT THE clock I saw it was 4:50 in the morning. I was alone in my bed and noticed I was wet. I got up and wondered if I had accidently wetted myself or if my water had broken. I paged my husband several times wondering how I would make it to the hospital if he didn't call me back...

127

I was 24 years old having my first baby. It was also the first time I experienced a miracle, at least the kind that you experience from a place of awareness. It wasn't just a miracle because I was birthing another human being, but because from where I was in my life at the time, giving birth to my daughter was the miracle I needed to change my life.

This is not the story of a woman who gave birth, went home, and was in awe and in love with the miracle she had delivered. This is the story of a woman who, through the miracle of her daughter's life, began to realize that her own life was precious and worth living.

Miracle, as defined in the Merriam-Webster's dictionary is: *an unusual or wonderful event believed to be caused by the power of God.* To me a miracle truly is caused by divine power—the power that is inherent within us and in the universe.

Awareness Awakens our Senses to Be Present with Life

IF WE WERE TO be in a constant state of awareness, we would notice that miracles actually happen every day, all the time. What doesn't allow us to experience this daily occurrence is our own limitations and belief that we are not the miracle created by source.

In my own life, I did not see how amazing I truly was. I lived like a victim for the most part and aimed to please. I wanted to be loved and to know I mattered. Even though I grew up with lots of friends who loved me and who were

128

always there for me, I didn't believe that I was worthy of their love or friendship.

When something good happened, I waited for the other shoe to drop. When I was in a relationship, I tried my best to please, and if I had a guy who actually treated me nicely, I backed away.

Of course, there were many great things happening for me and to me and sometimes I would be in my heart enough to appreciate them.

My intention as you read my story is that you discover you, too, are a miracle... that your life is worth more than you will ever know, and when you surrender to self-love, set intentions, have faith, and engage in prayer—you can manifest the greatest miracles in your life and have the kind of life your heart desires.

My Story

WHEN MY DAUGHTER was born I was living in my own perceived hell. I had wanted so desperately to have the perfect marriage I had seen in the movies and read about growing up. My life was far from a fairytale. My husband and I were constantly fighting and we both looked for each other to fulfill the hole we felt in our hearts. We were co-dependent on each other for our happiness.

I had lost myself completely. I had forgotten my dreams, my sense of self, and my purpose. Or better yet, those things I thought were my dreams and purpose, and who I thought I was, had shattered. All that remained was an empty shell. Although, on the outside I was still able to hold it together and successfully wear my happy mask, inside I was slowly dying—holding on to a thread of hope that was strong enough to stick around. I had no idea what it was like to thrive; all I did was survive each day.

The first time I became shockingly aware of what was really going on inside of me was when I was driving down the freeway and the thought of letting go of the steering wheel crossed my mind. A million thoughts flooded my brain, from *I'll show him what it feels like to feel guilty if I were to die*, to, *If I were to die, then he would be raising our daughter and I can't let that happen.*

A few times of thinking that way was enough to make me realize something was very off with me. I was depressed and weak and yet I felt something start to shift within me.

Encountering the Buddha Within

WHEN MY DAUGHTER was first born, I had decided that I was going to start a spiritual practice and I chose to practice Buddhism. At that time, my mother-in-law was a Buddhist and she had urged me on several occasions to chant so that I could transform my situation and my life.

Fortunately, my heart and my soul somehow knew that I needed a breakthrough and my daughter was the catalyst. For my daughter's sake, I began attending meetings and chanting. At first I didn't notice any difference since my life looked the same on the outside—I was still fighting with my husband, I still felt disconnected, and my environment still looked the same. But deep within, something was moving and gaining momentum.

Slowly, I began to experience courage. I could feel my heart opening and I noticed I wasn't getting as aggravated by the shouting and yelling surrounding me. I knew something was happening, but I couldn't quite put two and two together. The more I chanted and attended activities with my Buddhist group, the more I began to feel centered. I sensed that I was tapping into a wellspring of inner wisdom and confidence.

My first step toward initiating change on the outside was to stop engaging in fights with my husband. Whenever he would start yelling and shouting, I would disengage and go out. I knew this was a first step for me to become healthy and start honoring myself. I didn't quite have the words to explain to myself what I was doing; it simply came from within and moved me into action.

My next step was to start seeing a family counselor. At first, I wanted this to be an activity my husband and I would do together, but he refused, so I just kept going. I needed to keep building my strength—both in myself and in my faith. By the time my daughter turned one, I had developed enough courage, strength, confidence, and faith to know that my marriage was ending and I would start a new life on my own.

The second time I experienced a conscious act of a miracle was after I divorced. I was now a single mom, having no idea how I would afford to feed, clothe, and shelter the two of us. I needed to become a conscious manifestor—someone who couldn't just wait to be rescued but who needed to develop faith in her own power.

Being a single mom turned out to be one of the most transformational periods in my life. It was during this time that faith and trust became my bread and butter. At the same time, I became aware of how disconnected I was from my daughter. I had spent so much time surviving that I forgot to develop a relationship with the very child I had mothered.

I remembered attending a women's conference when she was two years old and going up to the mike and sharing in tears how awkward I felt as a mother. Here I was a mother and I couldn't relate to motherhood. I couldn't love this child because I didn't know how to love myself.

As I stood there pouring my heart out, I began to feel strength rise from within my life. I vowed that I would become the best mother my daughter could possibly have. I vowed that I would transform whatever fears, doubts, self-loathing I had going on within me and I would be the greatest example of womanhood possible for my daughter. I had no idea what that looked like or what it would take for me to achieve it, but I knew yet another layer had been pulled back.

I went home from that conference feeling refreshed and determined...

I had set my life in a forward momentum. I increased the time I spent chanting and studying. I began to really stay present in my self-talk, especially in front of my daughter. I also began to look at my daughter as someone who had so much to teach me. If I yelled at her, I would stop, breathe, give her a hug and say I'm sorry, and let her know that I was trying, but it took practice to change certain behaviors. Even though at a conscious level she may not have been able to fully grasp my words, I know that her soul was getting it.

I knew the part of this healing journey that began with my daughter's birth was to **learn how to love myself**. I knew that self-love was the key that would unlock my heart and soul to manifest the life I desired. I began designing my life.

Everything I did became intentional. I began to write down my intentions and dreams for the future. I re-enrolled in school. I started having dates with myself. I sat with my daughter and watched her favorite videos. I had sleepovers with my best friend.

Then finally at the end of that year, while writing my intentions for the following year, I began to realize how much my life had changed. I noticed that I no longer needed someone to make me happy. I noticed that my bad temper with my daughter had subsided... and I was the happiest I had been in years—truly happy.

I had written as one of my intentions to finally meet someone because I felt ready to be in a relationship again. This time, however, I was inviting in a partner who would see me as a whole person... someone who respected me as I had learned to respect myself... someone who was able to see and support my visions and dreams.

An Encounter with Love

A FEW WEEKS later I was at a New Year's Eve party and ran into an acquaintance who was in the same faith organization as I. We began to talk and that night, on that first kiss, I had a feeling in my heart that I had met the partner I had invited through my intention setting. I felt those amazing fluttery feelings in my belly, and like a young girl in high school who found love for the first time, I said to him, "Hmmm... Jackie VanCampen... I really like the way that sounds."

Yes, he did think I was nuts and probably wanted to run for the hills, but he stuck around and eventually realized that the feeling was mutual. Almost two years later I became Mrs. VanCampen and my daughter welcomed another dad in her life. And together we lived happily ever after...

After The Happily Ever After

THIS IS NOT the fairytale kind of happily ever after. This is the kind that we have to keep growing and expanding, and with growth and expansion come growing pains, doubts, and disagreements. It is however, the willingness to go through the process that makes for the happy part. And that's exactly what we have done in our own lives as individuals and as a couple. Is it easy? Not always, but it's worth it.

When my husband is losing it about something, it's my opportunity to ask myself what is it that he's reflecting back to me that I still have yet to transform. It's part of that self-love process and the more we go through it, the more we are able to manifest what we want in life. Why? Because the deeper you love yourself, the more courage you have to take action to actualize the life you desire.

As for my daughter, well, now I have three of them, and with my oldest who is now 16, I have the greatest relationship I could have asked for, and I truly feel I have become the role model of womanhood for her. This does not mean I'm perfect. It means that **I'm perfect in my imperfection** and I'm not afraid to be vulnerable and authentic with her. Through my own journey of self-love, I have been able to show her the woman I desired to be all those years back ... and I didn't even know what she looked like then. I'm still a work in progress, peeling more layers as I keep revealing more and more of my beautiful self.

Everything Begins with Intention

WHAT I HAVE learned throughout these years of going through my inner transformation is that everything begins with setting an intention and that intention followed by prayer has the power to move mountains; however, without self-love, it's nearly impossible to live a happy life.

You may have material things and wealth but be completely miserable and unhappy.

When we start to realize that we are part of the creation of divine source, we begin to see our value. We begin to honor the God within. Every day is an opportunity to set the intention to design the life we desire, but it needs to come from the place deep in us that knows how valuable we are. It needs to come from the place in our hearts that understands and knows who we are in our core.

I have had many experiences where I had to let go and trust that my wings would open or that I would at least have a soft landing. Not everything shows up just by us desiring it. It requires taking action and being patient while trusting that the seeds we have planted will blossom into what we desire in our lives.

Miracles are part of our lives and it really takes awareness to see them. The story I share here was just the beginning of many other stories in my life where miracles and manifestation occur.

When I set the intention of starting my own business and I decided to quit my full-time job to start my healing practice, I had to trust that everything would fall into place: my finances, my healing abilities, attracting clients, and my husband wouldn't divorce me because I was choosing to follow my heart.

There was so much energy of chaos around me from other people, especially from my husband for thinking I had lost my mind, and yet, I sat in prayer first. I had to stay grounded and centered if I were to survive the crashing waves around me and thrive. I then had to keep loving myself... all the way through the doubts and fears.

I believe the reason so many people don't manifest the life they desire is because they buy into their own and other people's fears. They doubt their ability to create because of past "failures." But if they were to look at the "failures" they would realize that they were mostly

136

stepping-stones for something better. When I am experiencing fear, I pull out my self-transformation toolbox and retrieve the tool that will help me with whatever is going on at the time. I consider myself a seeker and a student so I am always learning different tools that will help me along my path. Of all the tools in my toolbox, prayer has always been my favorite.

What I enjoy about prayer is that it allows me to draw energy and resources from infinite possibilities and it helps me stay grounded and centered as well as helping me tap into my courage and strength.

After I quit my job we ended up having to move to a new home in a new city because it made more sense financially for us. What seemed to be a downgrade, turned out to be the best thing that happened to our family. We ended up moving closer to my husband's work, into a cute house with a great backyard for the kids and our two dogs, and in a wonderful neighborhood with an award-winning public school.

I remember when we first moved I would walk at the park and watch as friends would walk together. At first I felt a bit lonely, but I intended to create bonds of friendship in my neighborhood. Within a year I had met some wonderful moms who became good friends, and now my kids and I can't even imagine moving out of our neighborhood. My husband—who had been so afraid if things would fall into place—realized this was one of the greatest things we could have done for our family. I now get to be home with my kids, volunteer at their school, and be an active citizen in my community, not to mention the great support we have from our new friends in the neighborhood.

It took reaching in and pulling out an incredible amount of trust to take action on fulfilling a dream. A dream is only made manifest when we can face our fears and take action despite them.

Enjoying the Gift of Manifestation

THERE WERE TIMES I would sit in my backyard and feel guilty that I was actually enjoying myself. One day, however, I became aware that I was actually living my life exactly how I had intended. I always wanted a backyard that I could sit in and enjoy the warm sun on my skin, to hear the birds singing, and to have a beautiful tree. There I was living exactly how I had intended and yet felt ridden with guilt.

Guilt is a pitfall to achieving the life you desire. So many of us feel guilty when we have success, money, healthy bodies, and harmonious relationships. We feel as if we are invalidating what our reality tells us how life should be. How can we be enjoying this level of (fill in the blank) when so many are suffering? How can we not? If more of us enjoyed our lives more and everything we have been able to manifest, the world would actually be a better place. We are so stuck in not wanting to make others feel uncomfortable with our happiness that we keep perpetuating the unfortunate cycle of lack, poverty, and suffering.

When I finally realized that my life had become exactly how I intended it to be, I rejoiced with tears flowing down my face, and gratitude so deep that I could not contain the happiness I felt in my heart. To think how much my life had transformed in those 16 years since I began my journey is simply incredible. It still brings joyful tears to my eyes!

When we learn to appreciate our journey and everything we have gone through, and where we are now in the present moment—even if it's not exactly where we have envisioned we would be—it's as if we open the floodgates of manifestation.

Gratitude is the partner of prayer. As we pray to create the life we desire, we must be in gratitude for what has come, what is now, and what's yet to come. Gratitude lets the universe know that we are present to the gifts in our lives, which in turn allows the universe to keep gifting us the desires that well forth in our hearts.

There is so much I still want to accomplish. I feel I have only begun. Every day is a new day filled with possibilities. I also know that as I keep moving forward there will be obstacles in my way, but I know that I have the power of intention and prayer to move forward, especially when I do so with love in my heart. Knowing that I am a child of Divine Source, when I honor myself, I'm honoring Divine Source and everything and everyone in the universe. When we honor and love ourselves, we know what our purpose here on this planet is and we allow ourselves to be moved by it. We become an instrument of love and peace in the world. When we live a happy life without guilt we are saying to Divine Source, "Thank you for these gifts. I honor them and I bless others with my abundance because I know that there is no lack."

The belief that there is lack is one of the greatest forms of control perpetrated against humanity. When we can release that belief, our lives become rich with ideas and ingenuity. We see how much knowledge and wisdom we actually posses and we can create sustainability for the planet and for its inhabitants. We don't need to destroy our earth; we don't need to create famine and diseases for population control. Instead, we can invest in renewable resources, education, and arts. Human beings have such a great potential to create an unfathomed life when we awaken to who we are.

I believe that is why I'm so passionate about helping people see their own greatness and light, because when they do, they can be such a tremendous contribution to the planet. I know because I've been in this place of lack and struggle and suffering. I've been shackled by millennia long limiting belief that we are not enough and as I break free from this belief, I see my life blooming. But it takes practice. It takes intention, determination and courage, and it takes being able to go within and practice listening to your own heart's wisdom and trusting it.

We have been conditioned to go without for answers even though we have the greatest form of intelligence within our heart space. It's okay to want to get confirmation or validation from the outer world, but, ultimately, we ourselves know what is best for us.

This is another lesson I had to learn throughout my life. I realized that whenever I go outwardly to find answers, I feel unbalanced and out of alignment with myself. I begin to question and/or judge myself, and my actions. There have been times where I would be so out of alignment I would have to seclude myself from the outside world, all the while, having to deal with the internal chatter that I wasn't good enough and that nothing I wanted was ever possible. In those times, prayer was my saving grace. I would meditate and journal and remember the many times in my life where I had been able to manifest what I desired. It truly is an exercise of self-awareness to catch the voice of the lesser self and do something about it.

Judgment, like guilt, is another form of control. When we judge ourselves, and others, we are saying to Divine Source, "I'm not worthy of being your child and I'm not open to receiving from you." Imagine if your child or a loved one came to you and said, "I don't want to receive your gifts or your love because I'm not worthy of it." How sad would you be? I know I would be profoundly sad.

Letting Go of Judgment

IT'S SO IMPORTANT we let go of judgment of ourselves. How can we empower our future generation when we are disempowered by our own judgments?

I used to unconsciously judge myself, until one day, my oldest daughter who was four at the time, came down the stairs, dressed in her Disney princess dress, looked herself in the mirror and said, "I'm ugly." I just about had a heart attack! I couldn't believe those few years of going through self-love growth had taught her nothing.

So I did what I always do, I asked myself where was I judging me? I realized that I judged my curly hair... I judged my belly, and other body parts. Of course, she thought she was ugly! That's the moment I decided that I would no longer judge my body and that I was going to love every inch of it: every curve, every dimple, and every ounce of flab, and as I did—I began to notice that my daughter stopped judging herself, too. I also started to feel so great about myself others began to see me in a different light as well.

Judgment is like a poison that kills off your potential for success and abundance. It leaves you feeling powerless, which creates apathy and resignation. We have been so accustomed to judging ourselves that to not judge feels unnatural. It takes practice to change this kind of behavior.

One of the things that helped me was joining a self-love campaign. A friend of mine decided to start posting on social media something she loved about herself. She decided that she was going to do it for 100 days. I thought it was such an amazing vehicle to move me out of self-judgment that I decided to join and invited several others to join me as well.

In the first week I had found several things that I loved about myself. It was going great until the critical voice showed up and began to tell me that I was just fooling myself. It had me thinking about what other people would think of me. It would find things to contradict that something I loved about myself. It told me, "You are wasting your time; after all, nothing will really change!" But... I stayed with it.

By the end of the 100 days, I had increased my self-confidence to a new level. I became so visible on social media I ended up attracting clients and many opportunities to be a guest on radio shows and eventually have my own radio show. In addition, many others had joined and someone ended up creating a group that we could go on every day and post in the group in addition to our own profile page.

This social media page not only changed my life, but it changed the lives of so many others. There are still people joining and others who decided to continue way past their 100 days.

When you love yourself, opportunities automatically come to you because you are open, visible, and vibrating at a higher frequency. It really takes just one person to start a train (chain?) reaction.

Will you choose to be that one person who will say yes to changing your life and paving the way for others to follow in your footsteps?

How Does One Pray?

SO, JUST HOW does one pray? Prayer is a very individualized action. Of course, you can pray in groups, but ultimately prayer is your communication with the divine. In addition to using a Buddhist chant as a way of prayer, I also meditate and have writing dialogues with my spirit guides.

There is no correct way of praying. I always recommend that one follows the direction of their heart, but I do believe that there are certain things you can do that can help you connect more deeply with your higher self.

Being in nature is a wonderful way to connect with the Divine. When we are in nature, we recognize the abundance that exists in the universe. Even in the desert there's abundance. Just look at the rocks and mountains and you will see abundance.

Meditation is a way to hear the wisdom and guidance of your higher self. When you go within and BE in the silence of your heart, you are better able to connect with your own inner guidance.

Journaling is a wonderful pathway to take the wisdom and guidance you have received and put it into physical form. Journaling is also a great way to give your soul a voice. I have developed a practice of journaling daily and when I look back and read what I have written, I appreciate how much wisdom has come through me, even during dark periods when I may be struggling with something.

However you choose to connect with your higher self, the most important thing is to **give your heart a voice** so that it may guide you through your path of creating the life you desire.

Everything that is showing up in our lives is of our own creation. So what will you choose? Open yourself through prayer, self-love, and intention and watch the magic of manifestation show up in your life in miraculous ways.

The moment you set your intention, every cell in your body begins to orient itself toward bringing forth the manifestation of your objective. You must, however, keep your resolve and trust that it is so; it will be. A tree doesn't become a full-grown tree in one day, so be patient as you tend to the manifestation of your desires and keep the momentum going. Anything and everything is possible. It's all within you. Isn't it time to unleash your own inner power?

About the Author

JACQUELINE VAN CAMPEN is a gifted healer and channel, using her gifts through her writings and mentoring program to inspire women to become Wise Heart Leaders in all areas of their lives. She guides women in accessing their Divine Feminine and heal through their stories.

The host of the radio show, The Writer's Divine Den on Positive Living Vibrations, and a contributing writer on various online media outlets, Jacqueline is also gaining favor as a poet as a contributor in the Spiritual Writers Network's newly released *Whispers of the Soul, A Poetry Anthology*. She is also the author of *Letters to My Daughter: A Mother's Journey of Healing* and the ebook, *Transformation and Wise Heart Archetypes: The Seven Levels of Awakening the Wisdom Within*.

This prolific writer and transformational messenger and founder of Wise Heart Within, Jacqueline is the mother of three creative daughters and married to her best friend.

Wise Heart Within Founder
Author, Writer, Radio Show Host
http://www.wiseheartwithin.com
jacqueline@wiseheartwithin.com
http://www.amazon.com/Jacqueline-van-
Campen/e/B00JLRNMSA

|Chapter 8

MOMENTUM THROUGH MANIFESTING AND MIRACLES

Anna Weber

When science, art, literature, and philosophy are simply the manifestation of personality, they are on a level where glorious and dazzling achievements are possible, which can make a man's name live for thousands of years.

~Denis Diderot

ARE YOU SKEPTICAL about the myriad possibilities of manifesting all that you desire in life and finding a few miracles along the way? It is quite likely the word(s) leave you hesitant – or   you are easily lured on a daily basis by quick thinking, fast-talking sales people promising to deliver instant results for something you desire! What would it mean to you, and how would your life be different if you learned how to tap into your desires and discover a manifestation process that becomes the essence of fulfilling the greatest of them?

Are you open to a different perspective—simply by having a deep and personal discussion about inspired abundance and how to achieve it?"

One of the greatest travesties of life is that many people have intense desires throughout their lives; few believe they can actually achieve them and have lives filled with quiet regret. Have you ever stood in awe and wonderment of those who embrace a life of inspired abundance... yet gave up on your desires and settled for comforting excuses?

Merriam-Webster defines the word manifest as:

1. readily perceived by the senses and especially by the sense of sight;
2. easily understood or recognized by the mind.

Other teachers of the wisdom of the ages may have inadvertently clouded a clear and simple concept—leaving us with the impression that there is something almost miraculous in being able to manifest something in our lives. You will...

1. read of the four-dimensions of manifestation: desire, direction, determination and discipline;
2. find what motivates you and how to recognize miracles in the midst of frustration;
3. understand the necessity of self-reward to effectively follow a success path;
4. embrace the power of strategic planning and the coincident actions that follow; and

148

5. cherish the results in creating a life you have always desired.

When you spend hours worrying how to manifest your desires, you break down both your resolve and belief that you are worthy and deserving of them. When your focus remains on *the how*, you are prevented from spending valuable time being actively engaged in the pursuit, and blinded to the opportunities and miracles that crop up all around you!

How are miracles defined? The World Dictionary notes:

1. an event that is contrary to the established laws of nature and attributed to a supernatural cause;
2. any amazing or wonderful even; and
3. a person or thing that is a marvelous example.

Have you lived most of your life not believing in miracles; perceiving them to be something strictly of a religious nature that pushes against your belief system? Might you be inspired here to take another look; miracles might be all around you!

Some people would have you believe there is a "best formula" for experiencing the rewards of manifesting and miracles; the only "best formula" is the one that works for you! It is based on your personal background, level of awareness, and experiences—all which come from your higher consciousness and allow the creation process to happen—unseen except in your results!

You have reached a point in life where this topic attracts you; perhaps it is time to open your heart to your desires and use simple tools to gain momentum in all you desire in life, through a rather simple process of manifesting your desires and learning to believe in miracles for all they are.

I have walked the journey you are currently taking, and in the process, discovered my life's purpose; my quest is to help others experience the kind of mind shifts I faced, allowing you to develop life skills and manifest your own desires. I am consistently confronted with amazing people who fail to reach their highest and best... because they lack sufficient understanding of myriad concepts you will read throughout this publication.

Since much of the success we experience in life deals with the business side of our lives, that remains my primary focus; however, foundational to all of that potential success, is my fervent belief business success is never forged from the outside—it evolves when you first address your inner game and grow a business that supports your personal core values and a chosen lifestyle.

It is only at this point of congruence, when life and business are in balance that you will free to add the momentum, experience the miracles and manifest your life as you dream it!

The Four Dimensions of Manifestation

SOMEONE ONCE INQUIRED why I chose the particular professional path of being a "Strategist," and I will never forget what spewed forth from my heart on that day! It made me profoundly sad to realize life is a beautifully amazing and precious gift that the most part... we waste. A travesty, directing me to help others find courage and direction to move beyond the "waste," and reach for the greater rewards offered by divine laws of the Universe.

Have you ever stopped to think about the unique and often-unexplainable challenges God sends your way... disguised as gifts? In the stories throughout this book, you glimpse others who, once recognizing the gift in their challenge(s), determined what to do with it, and used those gifts to finally live a life filled with passion and direction.

My "ah ha' moment... I came to understand there were even miracles in a career probating the estates of people who died in the streets... people with no family members to ensure that the end of their lives mattered! I came to grasp that my life's work involved being on the front side of life, not just wiping up the "waste." I was being called upon to provide direction and inspiration to encourage others to *get out of their own way*, as they sought a life free of self-limiting beliefs, fears, confusion, frustration, and disappointment.

My purpose and the steps I was to take became crystal clear! Design a process to identify the key principles of success, create individualized strategic plans, and serve as an accountability partner. I would come to serve others in manifesting their desires by teaching four success dimensions that included desire, direction, determination, and discipline.

I would like to encourage you to stop a moment and let your mind dwell on those four words—and get a sense of what they mean to you, or to recall if you have heard them through any other personal development work. For over twenty years, I lived a life in search of understanding myriad *universal laws of success.* I had grown to understand them, yet the sheer magnitude overwhelmed most of my clients; many exclaiming, "How am I to remember all these principles?" Strategically, my first step was to break down this large collective to a select few concepts that would be easy to understand on a daily basis.

Although each of these dimensions of manifesting your life can be approached independently, seriously consider there is a natural sequence. Is the following not a natural path we would follow in our quest?

1. Find your passion in life through understanding the dynamics of your *desire.*
2. Seek to find the fullest expressions of your desire by strategically following step-by-step *directions.*
3. Remain engaged in following those directions. Tapping into a personal resolve of knowing what exactly will keep you motivated, you will navigate beyond temporary setbacks and disappointments with a strong sense of *determination.*
4. The glue, so to speak, that holds you together in your quest is a keen sense of *self-discipline.*

I have to walk my talk! Remaining ever cognizant of quirky little philosophy that to get out of my own way, I must faithfully adhere to this same four-dimensional approach to becoming all that I can be.

My life's passion is clearly about sharing my education, experience, and skills with entrepreneurs who are serious about their own life transformation, and eager to engage in new forms of thought, behavior, and commitment in order to experience what may be deemed miracles! Granted, a very pragmatic, left-brain person—much of my work is focused around business plans, budget decisions, marketing campaigns, and other less-than-fun work. Gaining momentum in the quest for manifesting your life cannot begin in earnest until you invest a certain amount of time on your "inner game."

A strong premise: small changes made consistently create big results. A significant number of people seeking miracles in manifesting life and abundance stop short of achievement; overwhelmed at the enormity of the prospect, fearing the idea of changing what is currently comforting and secure, or not yet understanding how much they are actually capable of.

As Sir Edmund Hillary noted, *"The thing we must conquer is ourselves."* I would like to tell you there is a miracle in making this change happen; however, no one else can change your life. What I can promise... when you exchange being fully honest with yourself and courageous in making different choices—what may have previously looked daunting—will be seen as freedom, clarity, and purpose in place of confusion and doubt.

Desire

IT IS ESSENTIAL to elaborate a bit on the impact desire has on our lives; it is the foundation of all personal growth. With it comes the need to be acutely aware of *why you want what you want and what life will be like with the achievement!* If I were limited to exploring only one of the four dimensions to manifesting your life by design—it would have to be desire. With it, the other three will somehow fall into place; without it—you will always be chasing rainbows.

Let me boldly note desire is not primarily some romantic inclination. The best definition I could find was on Selfknowledge.com: *"The natural longing that is excited by the enjoyment or the thought of any good, and impels to action or effort its continuance or possession; an eager wish to obtain or enjoy."* Does this feel a bit nebulous? Does it refer too much to the emotional state you sense and feel? Stop a moment, consider this part of definition: *"and impels to action or effort its continuance or possession."* It is this understanding that compels me to include it as the first, most important element of manifesting success.

Is it possible the topic of desire causes you discomfort? Has time caused you to feel the need to hide your feelings of desire, just to avoid certain negative responses? A word of caution, too much avoidance and you may ultimately begin to hide your desires from yourself. Simply put... you cannot propel yourself forward without it! Consider the pursuit of an important goal you may have previously held. You look deeply at a plethora of possibilities and with an amazing sense of energy, you push through everything in your path—right to the edge of an imaginary cliff that represents your goal—and you have every intention of making a big leap. Alas! At the last moment you make an assessment of just how large that leap is and come to a sliding halt, replacing your joy and energy with fear and doubt.

"What just happened to me?" you ask yourself. You lost the depth of desire that would continue your forward motion and with that loss, you diminished the action and energy necessary to accomplish your next step. The real travesty is what happens next... once you allow the disconnect from your integral sense of desire to occur— you are now driven by far less compelling forces; passion is replaced by need and obligation, which are both far less empowering forces than passion.

Need and obligation will never outshine desire! It is *your why* that compels you. Stop and ask yourself, "Why do I want to generate more revenue? What is it about that goal that I really desire?" I am sure you will come to the conclusion that what you most likely desire is that revenue will provide—time, freedom, or perhaps security?

We all remember stories far better than concepts; they seem to cement the ideas in our hearts and minds. My "desire" story is of a man who wanted to lose weight most of his adult life—he just always got in his own way, never finding enough of a big why get him beyond the want—to the doing. Life has a funny way of teaching us lessons and this man's message came in the diagnosis of his only daughter with a life-threatening disease. The man fortunately tested as a favorable donor; however, under doctor's orders he could not participate in being a donor until he lost, at minimum, one hundred pounds. Needless to say, his *why* suddenly became large enough to match his *desire* to lose weight; what an amazing "rest of the story" that absolutely nothing stood in his way!

Have you ever looked around you—at friends, peers and family members, watching those who set goals year after year? Some people amaze you at how much they accomplish; others seem to be "put upon" by life's mishaps befalling them at every turn. What do you think is *really* the difference between those who never seem to *get it right* and people who always seem to get exactly what they want in life? It's—*desire!* You may argue, "I did set goals and had a strong desire and still didn't accomplish what l wanted." I would have to encourage being fully honest with yourself, and finding the clarity of where your desire ran short of taking you the full course!

I grasp concepts by mental anchors, and when it comes to the empowerment of *truly intense desire,* I have this vision of desire being a kind of mental "rocket fuel" that is so powerful you can feel a release of energy that simply boggles your mind. Words can do essentially the same thing. Consider the intensity of your own desire. Think about replacing the word "desire" with another word, such as "passion" or "conviction." Would one of those words create *truly intense desire*, where you remain connected to your goal 24/7? Imagine yourself... you are up early and you stay awake far into the night, never tiring of the energy to achieve your goal

Let me plant a seed in your minds of the odds stacked against Whoopi Goldberg, courageously moving beyond ugly, impossible life's circumstances to become an accomplished actress. What miracles existed for her? Had

156

she set in motion her own momentum, empowering an intense desire, dominating every conversation, thought, and action? Do sports figures manifest lives beyond limit, having a desire larger than the pain they know they will experience as they get in the ring or out on a ball field, having all nature of physical discomfort?

Understanding the dynamics of desire is not quite enough! You would have to agree, the concept begins in your heart and mind, and once you accept it as reality, then you are open to letting it take control of the patterns in your behavior and impact your thinking processes. One of the myriad "principles" is that as we consistently and systematically think a thought, over and over again, that thought becomes a habit—forming a "track" in your minds. If you rarely held that thought, the reality is your thought could quite easily be forgotten.

With the visions again! I was raised on a ranch, and think about the cattle trails—easily formed in the land around my childhood home. What I saw as a young child was   cattle taking the same trail, day in and day out, forming a distinct path; that path became a deep trench with the passing of time. However, when the cattle walked randomly through the fields, we could barely see where they had crossed.

With this mental vision anchored in my mind, it was easy to conceptualize just how desire takes over for us, and being entrenched in our hearts, the idea is stuck in our minds and the path we take becomes clear. At the point, our visions mesh with our desires, we begin an almost miraculous manifesting process.

157

The shift in a belief in miracles and your ability to quickly manifest the greatest desires of your heart is a **feeling...** you move beyond a cognitive awareness of a concept, and find yourself filled with passion and conviction. What is your task now? Keeping your desires burning with the depth of passion, actually breathing life and vibrancy into you. Gaining momentum as you openly embrace emotions and expressions, you see and feel details that intensify your yearning.

Desire is what fuels successfully manifesting anything in your life. I can promise you amazing results if you embrace and intensify your desire; without it, I can pretty much declare you will achieve very little of what is possible! Let's go back in history to the military leader who took his soldiers to battle, traveling aboard a ship. Imagine the chagrin of those soldiers, when—upon arriving at the place of battle, their leader ordered the ship burned. You may ask, "What was he thinking?" Probably to emblazon in their minds an intensely passionate reason to win the upcoming battle. You might also want to consider the vast number of athletes around the world... driven by their passion to succeed. The mere idea of taking an Olympic medal home did not suffice; each maintained a *burning, intense desire to succeed in their sport!*

Would you agree the stronger your desire, the deeper embedded is the degree of persistence; an underlying reason to support strong desire is a significant key to manifesting your goals. Not so important is the number of times you have failed; it is the number of times your intention is clear enough and *your desire strong enough*, that you try again and again. What separates those who do from those who do not succeed is the speed at which those

158

who simply *wish for success* give up in the face of adversity. It is when you are hungry and thirsty for success you find the direction and passion to persevere in spite of obstacles. You will be in possession of the intensity of desire that fuels in you a powerful, internal, and unstoppable drive.

Direction

LEST I SEND the wrong message—desire is only the beginning. However, once you have connected with one that you feel worthy of pursuit, the direction you take will certainly impact the momentum to be experienced.

The focus on *direction* is more about where you are going and how easily and quickly you are going to get there. Sometimes, if you are separated from the direction, it can be viewed as a self-imposed cage—blocking the ability to be focused in the right direction. I best explain direction as *putting in place a plan so specific the desired change will happen.* Wanting to keep you focused on the "inner game" I will gloss over this section a bit; it is the plan you create and the action steps you take that will change you from a state of "wishing" to a state of "manifesting!" With that thought in mind, I want to convey what I deem four necessary factors to ensure the direction you take will result in achieving the desired goal: knowledge, skill, attitude, and strategy.

Knowledge—Gaining the level of expertise necessary to accomplish your goal requires being aware of what you need to learn and what you need to have so that you might

159

learn most effectively. Time is not on your side if you want momentum; knowledge is!

Skill—It is at the moment knowledge is utilized to create effectiveness that it becomes valuable. You will learn to recognize the effectiveness is as you apply new knowledge and develop new skills. Cliché but true, "The more you do something, the better you get and the easier it becomes for you." Can you imagine your efficiencies once a task becomes second nature to you?

Attitude—Ah, this takes me to the inner game you must embrace! The most important of all four elements, you can rest assured nothing else spectacular happens without the right attitude. And it is through exercising confidence, courage, and persistence your attitude reaches the "altitude" of the highest mountain you hope to climb.

Strategy—I have experienced far too many people living their lives like an amoeba. Scientifically speaking, the are "unicellular organisms having no definite shape." The fascinating thing about them—relative to our human nature—is they have the tendency to spend their time reacting to the environment around them. No conscious design for their lives. The lesson: If you have no strategic plan of action, your accumulated skills, wisdom, knowledge and right attitude will be for naught. Until you take strategically designed action steps—what can you really expect to happen—short of reacting to life around you… as it happens to *you*.

Strategies are personal; they are individual and must be crafted in a manner befitting you and the miracles you want to manifest! The clarity you need, the direction that is so critical—there is no way around it. I have seen some people flourish on a one-page strategic plan; others required something more complex. But for now—the important thing is that you understand the value and how strategically planning the direction in which you are headed will impact the momentum you may experience.

Determination

DETERMINATION IS SOMETHING that is distinctly internal and requires endorsing your actions at a very high level of personal reflection. Only at this level of self-control can you experience a sense of freedom to do what's interesting, personally important, and vitalizing. I didn't spend twenty-plus years of studying the ins and outs of personal development, without realizing determination has given me the greatest room for personal growth.

As I was trying to categorize so many success principles, my heart centered on the word "dedicated," feeling it conveyed being positive, optimistic, and somehow—more action oriented. By its very definition, dedication is *"to immerse oneself with sincerity into a certain subject or properly setting apart of anything by a solemn proclamation."* Awareness stepped up and tapped me on the shoulder one day as I sought to take a client deeper in manifesting a gigantic goal. Can you imagine how receptive and open-minded I had to be in creating what would be my own life's work? There was a very "loud" moment when I realized how much of my work is involved keeping others deeply *engaged in activities* that keep them moving forward. I need for you to engage in something at a much deeper level than *solemnly proclaiming* what you want!

The shift I had to make is just another example of life showing me some little miracles that have a huge impact on the community I serve. This particular day I was in a state of being really frustrated on *behalf* of a particular client and direct from my mouth came a very loud proclamation, "I am just flat *determined* that I will work until I get the key for his positive change!" It was at that moment I discovered a significant difference—my life purpose involves promoting a totally different mindset to those who are in pursuit of manifesting their life desires... the focus was not on dedication but a more soul-felt level of determination!

Back to the drawing board; shift my focus to conveying the understanding of this totally different dimension— *determination.* Research showed me the key. According to the encyclopedia, *determination is "the act of deciding definitively and firmly to be firm or fixed in your intention to achieve a desired end, fixing, or finding a position, magnitude, value, or character of something, and the direction or tendency toward a certain end."* Within these words I found new power and passion... the conviction, and the directions that supplement my helping others in pursuit of a certain objective.

Whether your quest is for freedom of finances, time, health, relationships, or even just a general desired lifestyle, I would pray you will resonate with the phrase, *"fixed intention to achieve a desired end"* and come to believe firmly in the power of focused determination. How powerful and effective can you be if your determination is founded *"fixing or finding of the position, magnitude, value or character of something."* My hope is it will take you to an understanding of the importance of being determined in your decision-making process when you are setting goals and objectives.

If I might posture one question to you right here, right now, "If you can't embrace the magnitude, value, or character of the things in which you intend to invest your every resource, how quickly can you then be enticed to just slip off track?"

The deep pain I experience in thinking of just how few people step into this place of miracles, momentum and manifesting fuels my passion! A story that is deeply etched into my heart is of a client, now in her mid sixties, who always desired to be a writer, but taking the "kind" counsel of her parents, she pursued a career path sure to provide a more comfortable living. Coaching with her for well over nine months I could not get her to "connect" with anything remotely resembling passion! Her sadness and her disconnect finally surfaced, and once she made the important connection between her *why* and her *need*, viola! She combined a *passionate why* with a *strategically designed plan* that did not overwhelm her and, determined to prove her parents wrong and experience the joy in life that she so desperately wanted... she happily reports successfully having written six exciting, inspiring stories she's free to share with the world.

Discipline

DISCIPLINE IS OBVIOUSLY a very important element in manifesting the life you want; helping you control your actions and stay focused. In your greatest moments of personal honesty and objectivity, you must address the level of commitment you're willing to make in order to continue your journey to desired achievement. Lacking sufficient discipline necessary to remain actively engaged, you may just find yourself in a flurry, engaging in busy work that subconsciously takes you miles away from your plan.

Granted, you can speak of just how busy you are, and try to convince yourself what you are currently engaged is important, but you probably achieve little more than feeling overwhelmed. Imagine if you can, trying to convince yourself that you are just too busy to "stick to my plan." The result is not pretty... you fall into being like that amoeba and live the *life that comes at you*, rather than remaining in control of the actions which should be the core of manifesting a life by your design.

Intent on inspiring others, I often share quotes of wisdom with friends and clients. Some years ago, someone whom I was having problems getting the bigger message about discipline sent me a response one day. It came in big letters on my computer screen:

Discipline = Freedom

All those months and he finally *got it*—and even more succinctly than I had been trying to teach the message! It is unfortunate so many people view discipline as a nasty little thing in life designed to have an uncomfortable control over us. Fighting against it at every turn, we strive to keep ourselves in the driver's seat, so to speak, wanting the privilege to do whatever it is we are so selfishly inclined to do. Stop for a moment and ask, "How much more powerful can I be and how much more enriched can my life be if I just shift my thoughts to this simple statement—*discipline truly does represent my freedom?*"

Let me leave you with a list of freedoms to:

1. **make choices** that will transform our lives with positive sustainable benefits;
2. **live** an enriched life; and
3. **enjoy** even greater levels of just personal self-respect.

This list can be expanded; the choices are yours to make. The importance is making choices based upon long-term gain, and ultimately, combining desire, wisdom, and discipline with a strategic plan. Your reward is a life that moves you forward and sets you apart from others who are not willing to make disciplined life choices.

Recognizing Miracles in the Midst of Frustration

WE ASK FOR miracles, yet in the midst of the plethora of frustrations fraught in life, it can be difficult to recognize them. We know we have "done the work" and should be able to expect we have manifested our desires, yet continue to react rather than respond to the challenges. Consider how self-limiting beliefs impact the enrichment possible.

Unless, or until we let go of limiting beliefs, our process is repeating the same mistakes, hoping against hope that something will change—yet fearful that nothing ever will. How different would your decisions be if you were confident you could conquer your inner critic and eliminate self-limiting beliefs? What momentum would you experience if you had more control over the following limitations:

1. Success and wealth are things that belong to a limited few; I am somehow inferior to everyone else.
2. Some things just are not possible to the common man; only unique people can sail around the world, break the sound barrier, and put a man on the moon.
3. What I want to achieve may be too hard, take too long, or require too many personal sacrifices; one of the universal laws is that we must have an exchange for everything.

It is human nature to come face to face with limiting beliefs; it is absolutely necessary to identify and challenge them. These limiting beliefs will guide your every action and ultimately create your reality—what a travesty if that reality that does not match your desires!

When it is difficult to recognize the miracles we manifest —or to experience the momentum that keeps us hopeful, directed and focused—we need to step back and assess the potential in seeking the miracle of becoming our personal best. Start with recognizing a deep, unfulfilled desire, and take the next step—look inside for answers. One of the greatest miracles is to accept there is value in all we experience; good or bad. Through experiences we do not immediately recognize as a miracle is learning to control and create richly beautiful lives.

Momentum in your life's journey does not simply happen to you: *it happens as a result of all you do.* Accepting that you alone are responsible for your life, you actually begin to awaken your inner strength, and you begin to create and change your destiny.

Not having a solid explanation about why you have not previously been able to accomplish your goals stalls you; it is never about a lack of skills or knowledge or even the lack of hard work and effort. It is about not being able to look inside yourself to find what's actually creating a metaphorical *tug of war* between proclaiming your desires and actively pursuing them. It is the proclamation and pursuit of your desire that opens your mind and heart to the miracles that do occur.

After thirty-plus years of studying highly successful people, I'm confident that successfully manifesting your desires comes through change; change stimulated by embracing and applying success principles, together with opening to self-awareness. When you are clear about who you are and what you so richly desire, all change is easier. As discussed earlier, success is always an inside job—it starts with telling your *truth* and being clear about who you are and what you most desire in life. After that—prepare for the excitement of impending miracles as the principles, tips, tools, and support from others will make your quest an exciting journey.

You can keep your journey as simple as the four primary dimensions of successful manifesting discussed, or with a strong and open mind, expand and evolve as much as you feel capable. The end result is discovering your inner strength... in the process of embracing miracles, momentum and manifesting.

The Necessity of Self-Reward

MY INTENTION IN sharing stories is not to divulge confidences, but to clearly make the point that when you speak of manifesting success, it's not always about how much revenue you generate or number of material frills you add to your life. However, there must be some type of self-reward—there simply must! Sometimes it's finding the courage to journey down an unconventional path that will bring you the greatest joy. So, if you find yourself at a crossroad where you're seeking more success in life, then you must know for yourself what it is that will provide the intrinsic feeling you have ultimately been rewarded for your quest. In the end, I would wish for you that wisdom prevails, and where success is seen as a passage in mastering yourself, your thinking, your actions, and ultimately your mindset.

I had to address these same issues myself—and not come up short or wanting. What part of my passion for bringing these four dimensions of success to the world stemmed from my innate belief and understanding? How do I deliver the truth that unless you have a strong *desire* to attain, and you are *determined* to achieve a specific ultimate purpose, there is no real effort that you will ever put into that goal or objective? How do I shift you to understanding that when you lack engaged effort, essential actions are not strategically taken, and goal-oriented tasks are frequently replaced by mindless chatting, watching television, or engaging in busywork that provides no reward.

Lesson: Manifesting the success you desire is not an event you can set on autopilot—it is the direct result of the how quickly and consciously you combine determination and desire to drive specific, well-calculated actions.

The Power of Strategic Planning

EARLIER, IN THE section regarding the four dimensions of success, I spoke a bit of the direction that comes from strategic planning. I would like to expound on exactly the impact planning holds on the dreams you seek to manifest, the community where you reside, and the world as you know it.

Desire, direction, determination and discipline... in the face of today's shifting economy, each plays its own part in driving success. Each day is a new tirade of people questioning themselves, "What if I can't achieve it?" or "What if the economy drags down my business?" It is not the economy of which we must be afraid; these questions are based on false assumptions behind which we hide. I fervently believe your outcomes will be significantly different if you accept the reality that more millionaires were created in down economies than at any other time in history. If you are the kind of person who is willing to look deep inside yourself and be *determined* not to "go down with the ship," you will stand back, look at the pain of your situation, and in creating something in response to your pain, manifest miracles!

169

The power of strategic planning is clearly visible when we encounter setbacks and refuse to give up. Having a clear set of directions helps us maintain the miracles of a childlike sense of curiosity and daring. These directions also help us look at setbacks and failure as a learning process—often revealing the most successful people have failed more times than they have succeeded.

When it comes to connecting with the idea of pushing through failure, we need look no further than the work of Thomas Edison. A man who committed his entire life to inventing products to make life easier for others; Edison *failed continually*. Just think about it—he failed over nine thousand times in his quest to invent the incandescent electric light bulb. In reality, failure was simply not a part of Edison's vocabulary; he held to a mindset of learning over nine thousand ways what didn't work. Pause to wonder, how far will you keep going or how many times you will experience a sense of failure without giving up? What would it take for you embrace there is no such thing as failure, just continued feedback and learning?

Cherish...

A PART OF my promise was to help you understand the need to cherish the results in creating a life you have always desired. We have the responsibility to connect with the four dimensions of manifesting as previously discussed; what must follow is to cherish what is brought our way!

The process is simple; the journey is not. We live in a culture where as children we are frequently placed in "mental boxes" being told what to do, how to do it and when to do it. The end result is the struggle we have in maintaining sufficient confidence and courage to engage in the actions necessary to manifest our desires. The critical characteristics of successful people are hard-won. Little in life is as easy at is seems and we will always encounter unforeseen challenges and problems.

I appreciate the honor and privilege sharing the gifts and primary principles delivered to me—to share with you. Well-known for frequently telling my clients that my place in the world is to shake up their thinking, I thank you for the opportunity to touch you. If the primary messages here resonate with just one reader, I will be forever joyful. It that number expands, my place as a change agent and my life's purpose will be fulfilled. It is my own ability to discover and ultimately embrace my own inner strength that allows me this privilege. If you are transformed through the messages in this book... in my chapter—what a reason to celebrate!

About the Author

A LITERARY STRATEGIST, Anna Weber knows the value of sharing life stories in the quest of bringing wisdom and positive value to readers and guides sassy Entrepreneurs and savvy Service Professionals through the oft-time confusing and overwhelming journey of becoming successfully published. Anna, the CEO and founder of Successfully Published, Voices In Print and Get Your Book Noticed, understands the realities of publishing, writing and marketing a book; having provided support to Debut Authors for close to two decades in an industry rift with constant changes and transformation. Anna, who also finds happiness in life traveling with her husband, and engaging in other creative ventures, can be reached at:

AnnaWeber@VoicesInPrint.com
http://www.voicesinprint.com
http://www.amazon.com/Anna-Weber/e/B0050BX6NW
https://www.facebook.com/Voices.In.Print
www.linkedin.com/in/annawebervoicesinprint/
https://twitter.com/MyVoiceInPrint

Contributors Listing

Antoinette Sykes | Transformational Life Coach
Bowie, MD
http://AntoinetteSykes.com

Amber Boswell | Health and Wellness Consultant
Plexus Worldwide, Inc.
www.linkedin.com/pub/amber-boswell/85/5aa/8ba

Mary Canty Merrill, Ph.D. (President & COO)
|Industrial/Organizational Psychologist
Green Village, CO
http://merrillca.com/

Mamiko Odegard, PhD | Love and Relationship Expert
Founder: ACTonLove™
Scottsdale, AZ
www.ACTonLove.com

Valerie Sorrentino | Life Energy Coach
San Diego, CA
www.valsgift.com.

Angie Toh | Peak Performance/Transformation Coach
Singapore
www.itransform.asia

Jacqueline Van Campen | Gifted Healer and Channel
La Mirada CA
www.wiseheartwithin.com

Anna Weber, MAOM, CLC | Literary Strategist
Chandler, AZ
www.voicesinprint.com

16421884R00112

Made in the USA
San Bernardino, CA
06 November 2014